Modelling Aircraft

Tim Laming

LONDON
IAN ALLAN LTD

First published 1987

ISBN 0 7110 1679 8

Published by Ian Allan Ltd, Shepperton, Surrey; and printed by Ian Allan Printing Ltd at their works at Coombelands in Runnymede, England

Contents

Front cover, top:
Hasegawa's 1/72nd scale F-4U Corsair seen in a flightdeck diorama.

Front cover, bottom:
Tornado GR1, ZA467 'FF', of No 16 Squadron RAF Germany. *This side view and those featured in the colour section are reproduced by kind permission of Squadron Prints. Copies of these prints (size 11¼"×17½"), and many aircraft side views are available from: Squadron Prints, 3 Torrington Avenue, Giffnock, Glasgow G46 7LT*

Back cover, top:
1/48th scale Monogram F-106 in Michigan ANG markings.

Back cover, bottom:
Esci's US Navy A-4 Skyhawk.

Preface

The humble plastic kit has really arrived at last! Although almost every child has played with an Airfix kit at some time or other, the true modelling enthusiast has long had to suffer the association between plastic kits and child's toy. Thanks to modern manufacturing techniques and the sharp rise in oil costs (which were directly transferred to plastic manufacturing), the typical model aircraft kit has become something far beyond a simple pocket-money toy, and at long last is a serious reproduction of a real machine. Now more than ever before the model enthusiast can really capture realism in miniature and the plastic kit industry is entering a whole new era. In this book I will explore the model aircraft hobby and describe some of the techniques involved in producing scale model aircraft. Aimed chiefly at the beginner to the hobby, you will not find too many technicalities in the following pages; instead, I hope I will give you some idea as to the possibilities open to the aircraft modeller, a few suggestions as to just what can be achieved, and some hints as to how to do it!

Whilst the content of the following pages is largely the results of my own experience, the models featured in the illustrations are mostly the work of my friends and colleagues in the International Plastic Modellers' Society without whom my interest in the hobby would never have developed. I must express my thanks to fellow IPMS members from the Sheffield branch who assisted me by providing so many of their plastic masterpieces for me to examine and photograph, and I am greatly indebted to Neil Robinson for his continual help and advice.

Tim Laming

Above:
This superb F-106 in $^1/_{48}$th scale from Monogram is one of the most accurate and detailed kits currently on the market. The decals, which have been used to show a Michigan ANG machine, come from a specialist sheet. The written and photographic details in the background add to the interest.

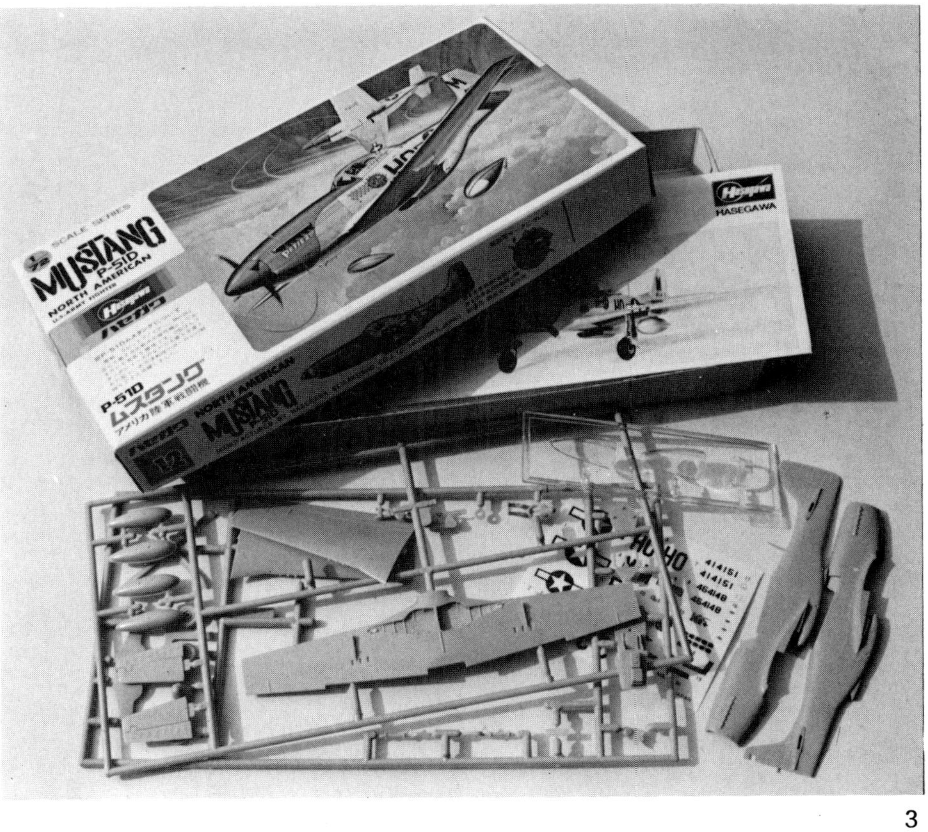

Right:
What you get: the contents of each kit box can vary widely, but as a general rule, the more expensive the kit, the better the quality and the more details provided. However, there ARE exceptions! On opening the box the very first job is to check that all the parts are included and are not damaged.

Getting started

Aircraft modelling is by no means a new hobby; indeed there have been attempts at creating miniature replicas of flying machines for almost as long as the 'real thing'. However, it was the introduction of plastic as a modelling medium which marked a major increase in the number of modelling enthusiasts. Until plastic arrived, wood was the popular material used to build models and although a limited number of talented individuals were able to produce beautiful scale masterpieces, the majority of model aircraft enthusiasts only began to become seriously interested in the hobby when the much more practical plastic arrived on the scene during the 1950s. Years earlier some initial attempts at aeroplane kits had been introduced. Most were essentially blocks of wood, from which the subtle shapes of the original were carefully formed by hand; however, a British company, Frog, released a series of kits which were the forerunners of today's products. Known as the 'Penguin' series, these kits were moulded in a Bakelite-type material and actually represented the proper shape of the aircraft they were portraying. The modeller simply had to assemble the parts and add refinements as desired. It was also at this time that the idea of producing kits to a common scale was introduced. Frog decided to manufacture all its kits to '$^{1}/_{72}$nd scale', which in those days was referred to as '6 feet to 1 inch'. This meant that the model would be exactly 72 times smaller than the original, and to this day this scale is by far the most popular and common, although other scales as $^{1}/_{48}$th and $^{1}/_{32}$nd are also fairly common. The reason that most kit manufacturers have adhered to the $^{1}/_{72}$nd scale size is because it allows aircraft of almost any size to be modelled without the completed model being either too big to handle or too small to appreciate fully. In the USA, however, $^{1}/_{48}$th scale is very popular, chiefly because the American modeller generally has more room in which to store his completed models. Of course, if you are new to the plastic modelling hobby you might think it is not really necessary to consider such things as scales, and whilst this might hold true for anyone who might only build one or two models, the situation is very different for those who decide to take up the hobby in a big way. There would not be much point in starting a collection of kits if they are all going to be of differing sizes, when it is quite possible to build a whole collection to a single scale. The results are much more interesting and graphically illustrate the differences (especially in size!) between various aircraft types. Even if you are only just starting the hobby, it is useful to remember such points when buying your first aeroplane kit.

Another aspect that is worth considering right from the start is the aircraft types you might decide to collect. You can choose between airliners, fighters, bombers, helicopters, World War 2, World War 1, British, German, American — the list is endless. However, it is important to remember that most military aircraft are produced in $^{1}/_{72}$nd scale and generally only smaller fighter-type machines are produced in the larger scales. Conversely, because of their greater size, the types of airliner kits available are almost all produced to $^{1}/_{144}$th scale, which is exactly half the size of the common $^{1}/_{72}$nd scale. It must also be said that the number of airliner kits available is by no means as large as the military alternative, and the variety of types is much smaller. The fact is that warplanes are consistently more popular; as a result, this range is by far the largest. It is unlikely that anyone with more than a passing interest in the hobby will build just a couple of kits. It is quite probable that you will continue to collect models and so it is wise to consider the scale, type or theme to which you are working. There is no reason why you should not simply buy whatever model takes your fancy, but for a more satisfying result there is nothing to beat a whole collection of models all built around a particular theme. Indeed, some modellers often collect just one aircraft type and prefer to explore the wide variety of paint schemes and markings, rather than different types. Of course, the choice is always yours, but you should think about these aspects of the hobby before you begin.

The constant improvements in kit quality makes almost every new kit noticeably better than the last, and those who have never built a kit before would be well advised to start with the most recent releases: in this the model shop assistant can often be of help,

A VC10 from an Airways vacform, with some smaller friends gathered around. All the models are to the same $^{1}/_{72}$nd scale and illustrate how a collection of constant-scale kits can show some interesting differences in size!

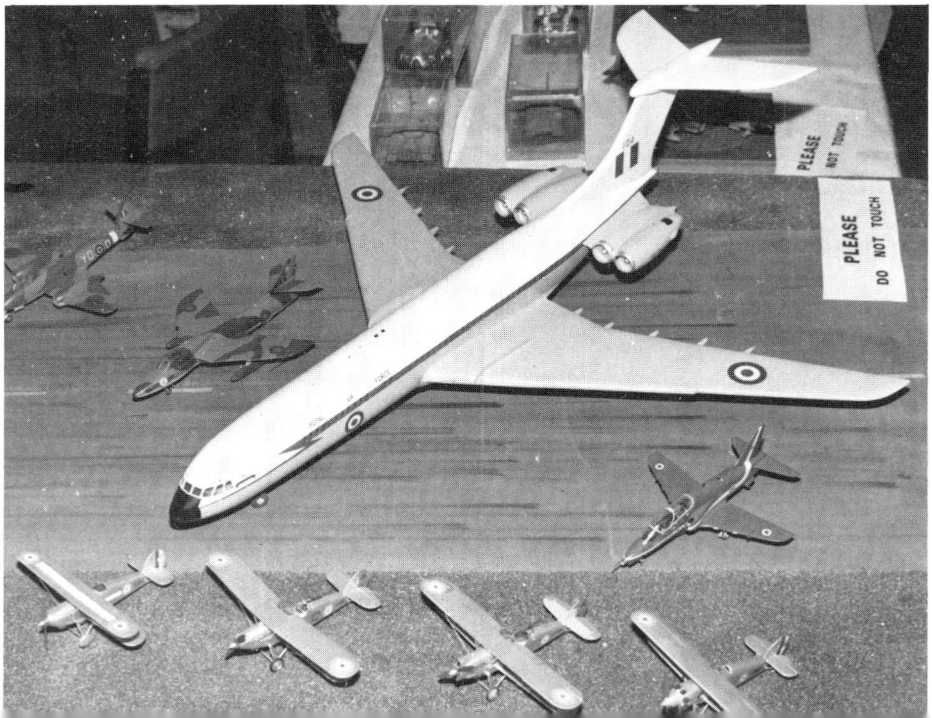

Above:
The elderly Frog Mustang, which is no longer available but can be found on specialist trade stands at modelling shows.

finding the latest kits. Those that are new to the hobby often fall into a well known 'trap' of buying an inexpensive kit to 'try out' on. This is a bad idea because the least expensive kits are likely to be the oldest and consequently they often suffer from very poor fit of parts, lack of detail, warped components, excess plastic covering smaller parts and so on. None of these pitfalls is likely to endear the plastic kit to the raw novice, and it is a far better approach to track down a new kit of high quality — admittedly quite expensive — that will be much easier to build and guaranteed to give a more encouraging end result. The fact is that the old kits are very much the property of 'experts'. Yet another point to keep in mind when buying an aircraft kit for the first time, is to avoid picking up the kit which is contained in the most attractive box! This might sound like an obvious rule, but it is surprising just how many people can find themselves buying a kit just because the box has a striking painting or photograph on the top. Of course, the box artwork bears no relation to the contents! It is always advisable to take at least a brief look at

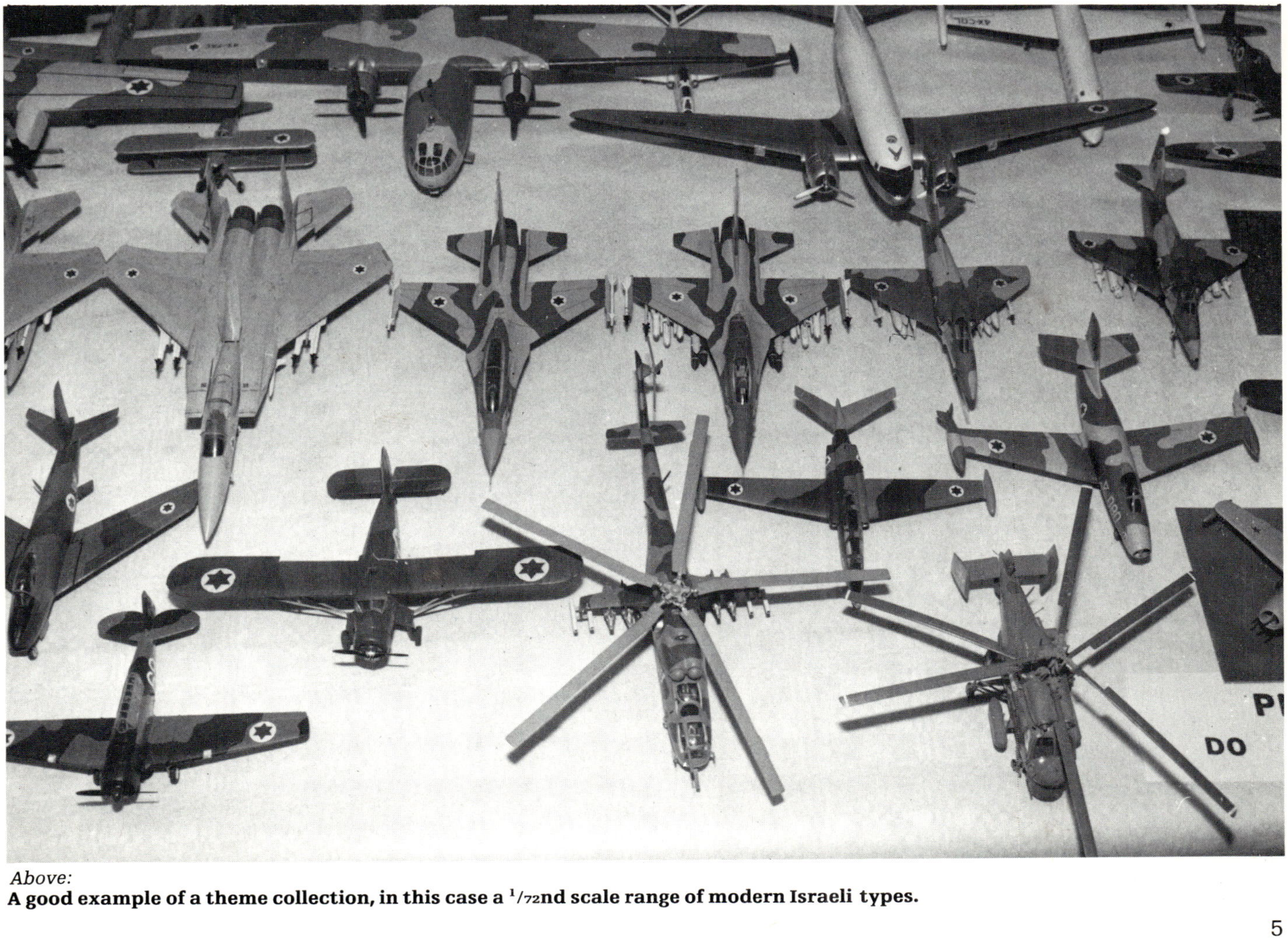

Above:
A good example of a theme collection, in this case a 1/72nd scale range of modern Israeli types.

A F-104 Starfighter trio: a QF-104 in a predominantly orange colour scheme (left), a Japanese F-104J, and an experimental German F-104G complete with an extra tailplane on the fuselage. All three are basically Esci $^1/_{72}$nd scale kits.

the box contents before making a decision. Understandably, many model shops actively discourage the opening of kit boxes to avoid the loss of small parts, but a sales assistant will often allow one to inspect the contents. You would not buy a book without first leafing through the pages, would you? Having purchased a kit, it is important that you do not open the kit box again until it is safely taken home and placed on a well-lit work surface, be it a table, bench top or whatever. Because of the many tiny parts contained in each kit, there is no way that one can be sure that all the pieces are going to stay in the box unless the lid is kept firmly closed. It is also wise to remember this fact when buying a kit. If the box appears to have been opened or damaged in any way, it is quite likely that some parts may have been lost or damaged — another reason to check the state of the contents in the store, before buying.

If you are new to the hobby, it is quite likely that you will not have the appropriate tools with which to complete the job. Like many hobbies, the number of tools and accessories that can help in construction is extensive; however, there are only a few basic items without which a kit cannot be easily built, if at all. The most obvious item is an adhesive with which to connect the components. In the case of the plastic kit this is polystyrene cement, which comes in two forms, a liquid (in a bottle) or a semi-solid type in a tube. Until just a few years ago the tube variety was the only sort available and so it is still commonly identified as the normal 'kit glue'; for the modeller's first kit, a better alternative would be the liquid cement (or indeed, both, as the cost is not all that high for either

Far right, top:
There are many tools which can be useful for aircraft modelling. The most important items are illustrated here, such as a modelling scalpel *1*, a modelling saw *2*, a small pair of sharp scissors *3*, a pair of tweezers *4*, a pair of pliers, which might not be essential but can have uses *5*, paint brushes of varying sizes and shapes, to suit individual preference *6*, abrasive paper *7*, modelling files and emery board *8*, clothes pegs (for holding parts together) *9*, a clamp (for the same purpose) *10*, and sticky tape and/or masking tape *11*.

type). Tube cement is inherently messy and is likely to 'string' into long trails of glue which sticks everywhere and generally makes the whole construction process a rather clumsy affair, especially when trying to stick tiny parts. The liquid variety, however, is rather like a bottle of water and can be applied by brush in tiny amounts. More importantly, any accidental drops of liquid cement will evaporate and cause little damage to the plastic surface, whereas the tube cement will gradually dissolve and 'burn' into the plastic.

Another modelling necessity is a pair of sharp scissors, ideally of the small surgical type. Large paper-cutting scissors or similar will be of little or no use and as a rule the smaller a pair one can find, the better. In addition to scissors, a sharp knife will be needed for trimming small pieces of plastic and cutting delicate plastic parts. The knife is an essential item and a kit can be ruined if a good sharp knife is not used. All hobby shops will have a range of hobby knives, designed specifically for modelling use. Some are quite inexpensive, normally made with a 'one-shot' blade (which cannot be replaced) and with a plastic handle. A much better buy is a proper modelling scalpel with a metal handle and an interchangeable blade. The blades come in various shapes and can be purchased for just a matter of pence; all can be immediately disposed of once they lose their sharpness. It is best to try a number of different blades to find which one you are most comfortable with and then stick to the one type. A good knife will last a lifetime.

Whilst not an immediate essential, a small file is always handy. A more practical purchase is some abrasive paper, which is ideal for quickly removing ugly joint lines or surface blemishes. Indeed, most modellers come to regard abrasive paper as an essential. Nevertheless it is important to identify the particular type of paper the modeller will require, as there is quite a wide variety available. Simple sandpaper is of no use: silicon carbide paper is the type the modeller needs. This paper is graded according to the surface texture, ranging from a very rough surface (likely to be of more use to a stonemason!) to a very fine finish with which a careful modeller can eventually learn to achieve a smooth paint finish on a tiny model. The average modeller will find that a selection of sheets graded at 200 (rough), 400, 800, and 1200 (fine) will be the ideal choices to cover most circumstances. One useful feature of this 'wet and dry' paper (as it is often called) is that it can indeed be used wet, which helps achieve a better abrasive quality (dry paper often clogs with plastic dust); the 1200 grade paper even gives a

Modelling Tools

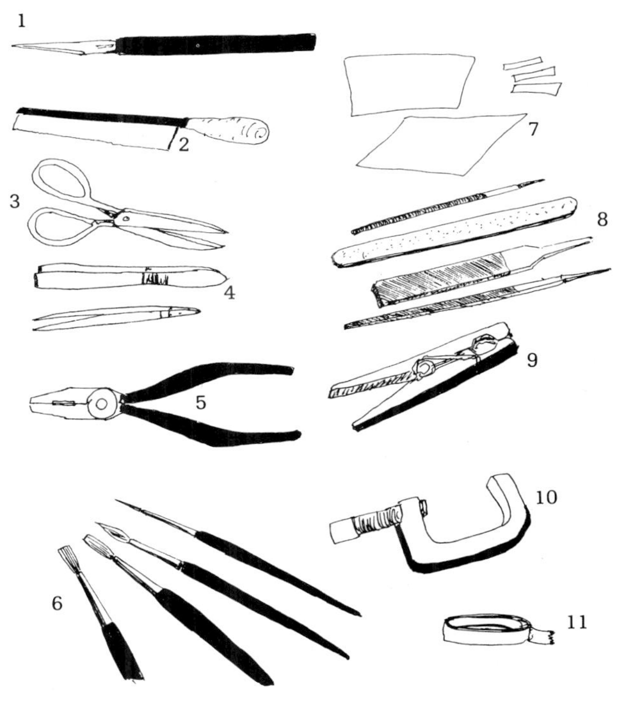

Top:
Starting from scratch: built completely from plastic card and home-made items, this is a fine example of just what an expert can achieve — a $^1/_{72}$nd scale B-45 Tornado.

Above:
Getting together with fellow modellers can lead to spectacular results. A group of Newark modellers produced this complete history of the Lancaster, tracing its development from the early Manchester, right through to the Lincoln and Shackleton designs. Spread between a number of enthusiasts, an interesting and informative display can be built up. The use of captions and photographs enhances the finished display.

Right:
A 'big wing' RB-57 Canberra with a selection of other '57 variants in the background, all built from the Matchbox and Airfix kits. A family of aircraft based on the same design makes a good modelling theme.

Above:
Two of a kind: a Meteor F8 built from a Rareplanes vacform kit (left) and a Meteor F4 from the older Frog kit.

good polishing effect if a little detergent is added to the water.

These are the basic tools for the job, but there are many more that will assist the modeller in achieving his ends. The beginner is probably best advised to avoid getting confused by the range of accessories available because the basic techniques of model-building do have to be learnt and no matter how many modelling vices, electric drills, electric saw cutters, magnifying glasses, etc, the modeller may buy, the simple task of fixing together the parts of a kit cannot be bypassed; even a world class competition standard model can be constructed with just some cement, abrasive paper and a knife, together with the most important tools — a pair of practised hands.

The basic tools for the job have to be obtained right from the start; and this is the time when another important decision has to be made; where are you going to build your kit? It might seem like a pointless question, but deciding where you can build your kit is almost as important as getting the right tools for the job. It is not advisable to tip the box contents on to a tea tray and immediately set forth. A light tray can be knocked over, with disastrous results. The dining room table is a better alternative, not least because there is likely to be some good lighting available there, which is always an essential in modelling. Unfortunately a table does have disadvantages, the most obvious being that mealtimes will interrupt the whole effort. Of course, another problem is that tables can be damaged, either by scratching or by spilling adhesives, which is a certain method of losing your entire family's support in your new hobby! The best alternative is to set aside your own table or bench, be it in your own room or in a garden hut: the location does not matter as long as it is somewhere that will allow you to leave your model undisturbed throughout its construction. Of course, there are many who simply do not have room for a specific modelling area, in which case a large heavy tray (with sides) used on a table will suffice, but it is important to protect the table with newspapers before commencing work. The heavier the tray the better (it cannot be knocked over as easily), but the most important feature must be the sides, which will stop the loss of small parts that would otherwise simply roll away on to the floor, never to be found again. Although you may think that a tray is the ideal modelling surface, do give every consideration to finding your own modelling table, as this is a much more convenient and sensible location which will pay dividends in the future. If you aspire to the realms of air brushing and kit conversions, you really have no option to finding your own modelling area, as the mess and smell associated with such activities will not allow you to work in any inhabited rooms!

Any table or bench would be best situated next to a window, which will allow the maximum amount of light to fall on to the work surface. It is vital that the area has adequate light — an adjustable lamp is best (if you can afford one) — the main point to remember being that the light must be able to shine directly over the surface (ie, where your hands will work) without being obscured by your body or head. Because of the fine plastic dust particles that often arise when sanding plastic, good ventilation is also a consideration, especially if you intend to proceed to the art of air brushing, etc. A window that can be opened wide is a good start, but an extractor fan is the most effective, but expensive, solution. The beginner's approach is to find a place where there is a good flow of fresh air. The history of plastic modelling is rife with hairy stories of modellers coming to grief, thanks to the inhalation of plastic dust and paint fumes!

Above:
The Airfix Bulldog (left) and Matchbox Fury, both to $^1/_{72}$nd scale.

Getting it together

Having chosen a model and set aside some time to begin work on your new kit, it is time to open the box and get started. Your immediate instincts will probably encourage you quickly to start sticking parts together, but a more patient and thorough approach is needed. Firstly, although it might seem a trifle tedious, it is wise to check the instruction sheet and compare the list of kit parts (which is normally included on modern kit instruction sheets) with the pile of plastic you have on your table. Check that the complete number of components is there, because if something is missing this is the time you should take the kit back to the place of purchase, not a few days after you have begun building it! Occasionally some instruction sheets will not give a complete breakdown of the contents of the kit, in which case a careful inspection of the plastic trees (or 'sprues') to which all the parts are connected should reveal whether any parts have been broken or lost. To be fair, most kits are sold in perfect condition, but very occasionally parts are missing. Sometimes one set of components connected to one sprue will be included twice, instead of the intended differing sprues, for instance, and a fault such as this becomes very clear when you find that there are two sets of right-hand wings but no left-hand set, for example.

Your next action might well be to remove all the parts from the plastic runner sprues, but this is an unwise step; whilst the parts remain connected to their sprue they will have an identifying reference number, which will relate to part of the construction sequence as illustrated on the instruction sheet. If the parts are all cut away there is no means of identifying any of the pieces, which can make things very difficult for you. Sometimes there are a few parts which have become partially separated from their sprues (through constant handling of the kit box, etc) and in this case there is no option but to remove the pieces; when doing this, a good tip is to stick each removed item on to a strip of masking tape on which you can also write the appropriate reference number. This will avoid losing items and ensure that you still know which piece is which.

Removing parts from the sprue carelessly can also present problems. All items must be cut from their plastic runner with a sharp pair of scissors or with a sharp knife. No parts should ever be simply pulled or twisted from the sprue, as there is almost inevitably a resulting amount of damage to the piece. Remember that no parts will separate cleanly from the sprue unless cut away. Once removed, the parts should be 'cleaned-up', that is the places where the pieces were connected to the sprue should be sanded or filed

Kit Parts

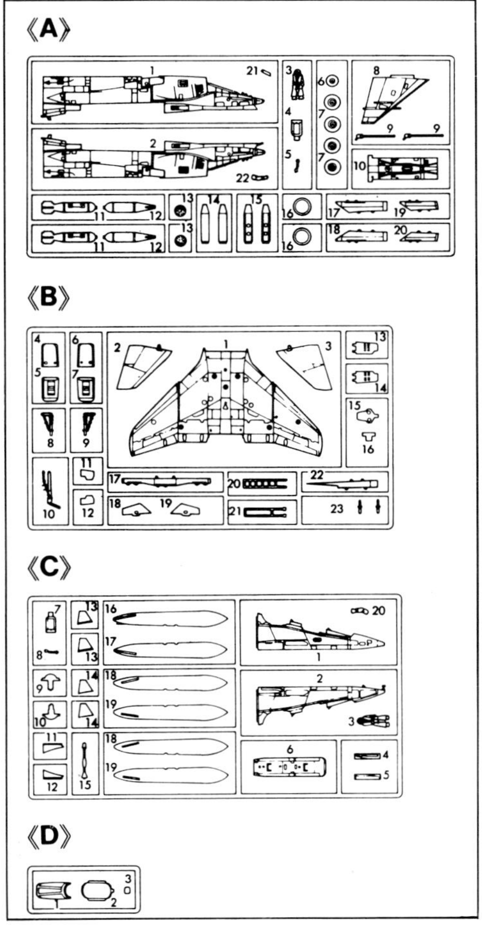

Left:
All parts come attached to their runner 'trees' (or 'sprue'), and will have individual numbers marked on the sprue, close to each part. Also, each sprue may have an identifying number or letter, and larger parts may have numbers marked on their inner faces. This illustration is from a Hasegawa $^1/_{72}$nd scale Jaguar kit.

Above:
An interesting Mystere IVa model, made from a combination of a Heller Ouragan and Airfix Mystere B2 kits. *M. Purchase*

Removing Parts

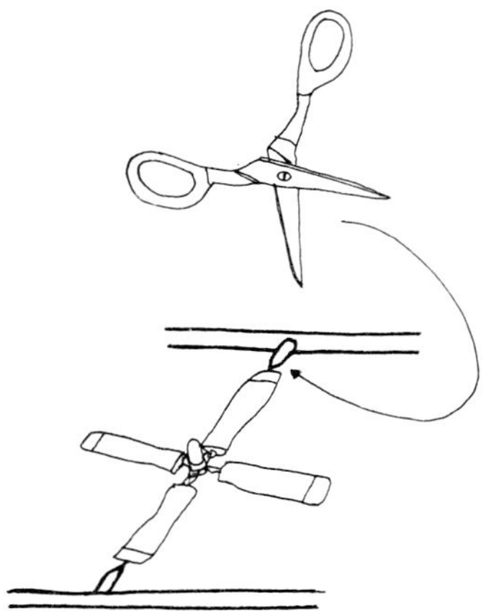

Above:
Parts should never be twisted from their sprue. A sharp pair of scissors will do the job much more effectively without damaging the pieces.

Small Parts

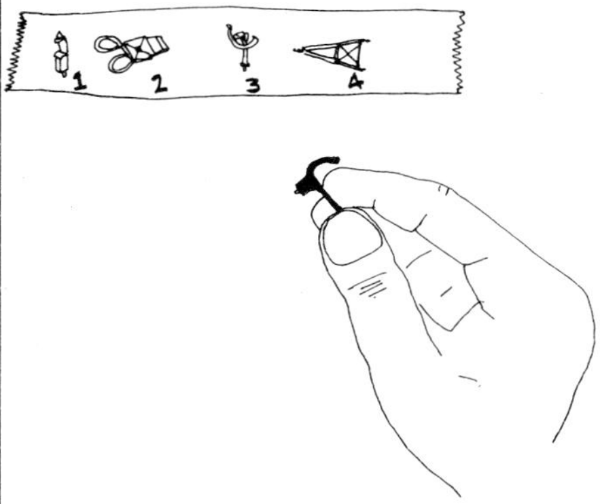

Above:
Small parts may have fallen from their sprues, in which case they should be kept in safety on a piece of sticky tape, on which you can also note their numbers.

smooth to their proper shape. On some small components, occasional pieces of excess plastic (or 'flash') can be found and these should also be removed with either a scapel or abrasive paper.

The next step in construction is to perform a 'dry run', during which you should temporarily assemble the major components to check for general accuracy. No glue will be needed, as the object of the exercise is to ensure that the major parts fit together as well as they can before any glue is applied — it is generally too late to take any remedial action should you find that any glued parts do not fit together correctly. During a dry run you can check that there are no bits of excess plastic obstructing connection and that all the connections to the sprue have been removed cleanly. Remember, once the glue has been applied, it will be much more difficult to correct such problems.

A dry run also affords you a chance to become familiar with the assembly sequence of the kit. You may find that your own preferences enable you to construct some pieces in a different sequence to that advised by the instruction sheet, although you must make sure that straying from the instructions will not create construction problems later in the building sequence. Perhaps another important benefit of a dry run is to confirm that the instruction sheet building sequence is completely accurate, as instructions can contain the occasional mistake. Before removing the majority of the parts from their sprues you should also consider whether any pieces would be best painted at this stage. Some parts will be difficult to paint when fully assembled (such as the inside of cockpits, wheel wells, jet pipes, etc) so you must think about this right from the start. Another point to remember is that some small parts will be much easier to paint whilst still connected to the sprue.

The most important stage of any kit assembly is that of cementing the pieces together. It is at this point that the modeller finds most problems, and many dustbins are filled with kits which have never survived this stage. Your first experiences in cementing plastic may have been rather messy ones, but with a little thought and practice you should not encounter any problems. One of the big contributors to many disasters is tube polystyrene cement. Novice modellers often underestimate the power of this adhesive and apply far too much glue to the plastic surface. This has many results: firstly, the glue oozes from the joints and runs everywhere. Secondly, the glue will not set for a very long time and, thirdly, the cement burns away the plastic. Unlike a typical contact glue, polystyrene cement welds the parts together by actually melting the plastic where it is applied. Consequently if too much is applied it will melt a large amount of plastic. If it is allowed to run all over the place it inevitably sticks to fingers which, in turn, transfer the cement to other clean areas of plastic and so on, until the whole model becomes a sticky mess. It must be remembered that only a small amount of cement is needed to do the job. Thankfully many of these problems were overcome with the advent of liquid polystyrene cement, which is applied with a brush. With this cement (which has the same consistency as water) you can apply tiny amounts to precise places. Another advantage is that you can hold two parts together whilst simply running your brush (coated with liquid cement) along the joint; the glue will run into the joint by capillary action. The other big advantage is that liquid glue will

Trimming Parts

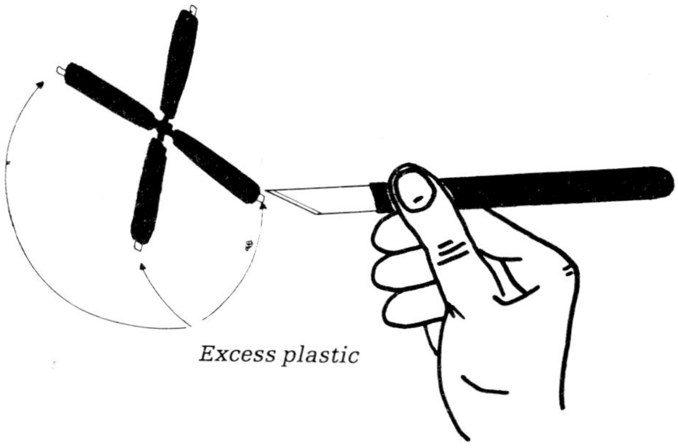

Once cut from the sprue the pieces will have small attachment points which need trimming with a knife.

Dry Runs

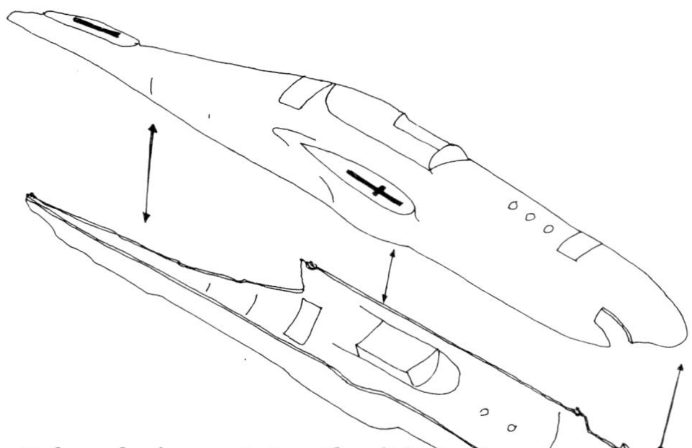

Before glueing parts together it is wise to check with a 'dry run' that the respective items DO actually fit together. You can save much work by finding parts that may need cutting or sanding before the glue is applied and the whole task becomes messy.

dry much faster (because it is so much thinner than tube cement) and consequently is liable to make much less mess.

Many liquid cements are sold in bottles which contain an applicator brush in each lid. In every instance the brush is far too large for proper modelling usage and should be ignored. For the delicate art of plastic kit construction you need a small brush with a thin head that will allow you to apply cement in exactly the right place. An old paint brush of suitable size is the most simple answer to the problem, but if you are just starting modelling you will probably have to go to a good hobby shop or an artist's shop to purchase a small brush, which should last you for a very long time. There is one point to remember when buying a brush for glue, however, and that is to check at the time of purchase that the bristles will not melt when dipped in polystyrene cement!

Whilst advocating the use of liquid cement, it must be said that the tube variety also has its uses. It will come in handy for cementing large pieces (such as fuselage halves) where liquid cement will often dry before the piece has been covered adequately in all places. The tube glue, being thicker, will not dry as quickly. When using tube cement in any circumstances, it should never be applied directly from the tube. It should be spread carefully with a cocktail stick or pin. One further mistake made by many novice modellers is to use tube cement to fill gaps between joints. This is far from wise, because although the glue may appear to fill gaps well, it will gradually melt the plastic and cause great damage. All gaps should be covered with a specific model filler, never with glue.

Once any major pieces have been joined together with cement they should be held together either with elastic bands or sticky tape and be left to dry thoroughly. Quite how long any joint takes to dry depends on its size and how much glue is applied. There are no definite times in which glue will have dried, and the most sensible approach is to leave parts for as long as possible, once glued — and in the case of large parts we are really talking about a day or so, rather than hours. There is always a strong temptation to work on a kit before parts are completely cemented together, but this temptation should always be resisted because the result of hasty construction is almost inevitably a disaster of some sort, which will either create even

Using Liquid Cement

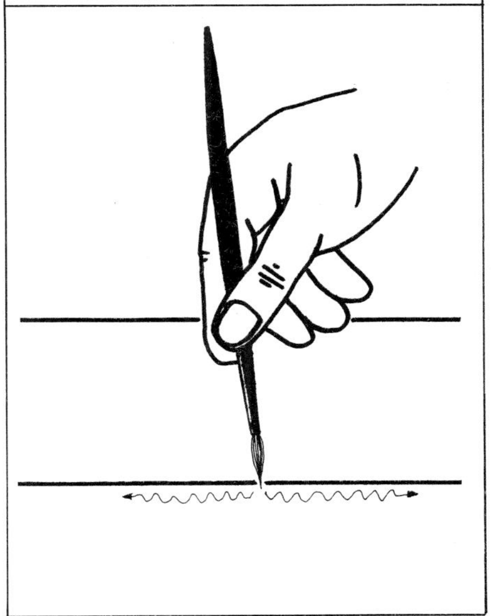

Above:
A spot of liquid cement applied to a joint line will run a considerable way along the joint due to capillary action.

Holding Parts Together

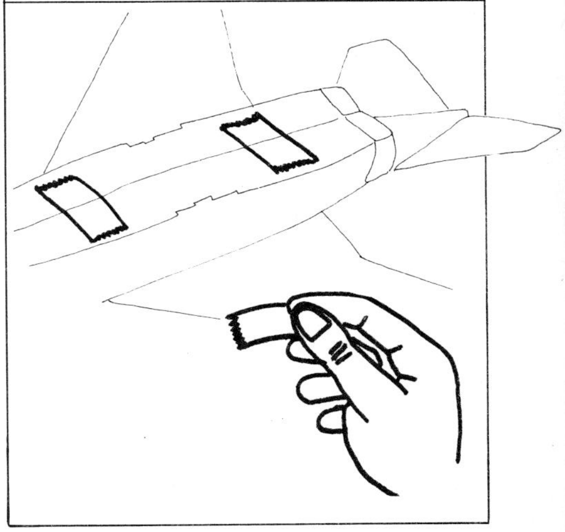

Right:
Many parts need to be held together while the cement dries. Sticky tape will often do the job, as will a vice if it is used carefully so as to not damage the plastic. Elastic bands will also help, and clothes pegs will secure parts such as wing halves.

Below:
Attaching small parts to the model can be an awkward task, resulting in glue on fingers, model and everywhere else. A pair of tweezers will save you much mess and trouble.

Below right:
Parts such as undercarriage need to dry thoroughly without being touched. Standing the model on a box will allow the gear to hang down without touching the floor whilst drying.

Using Tweezers

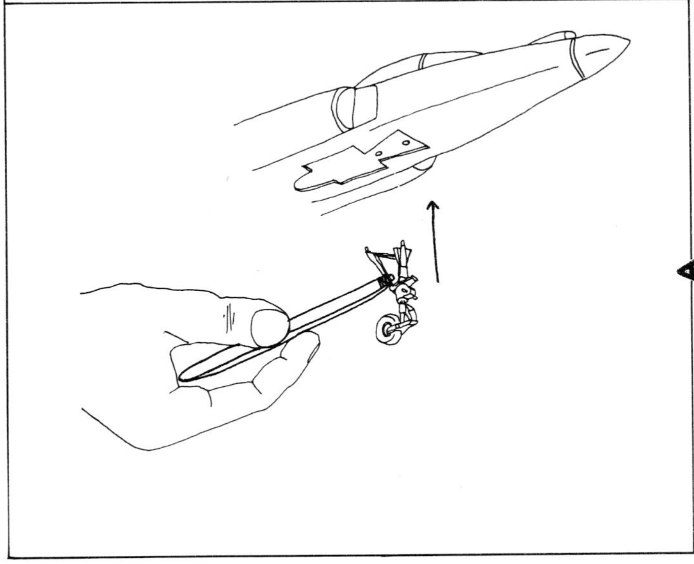

Drying Delicate Assemblies

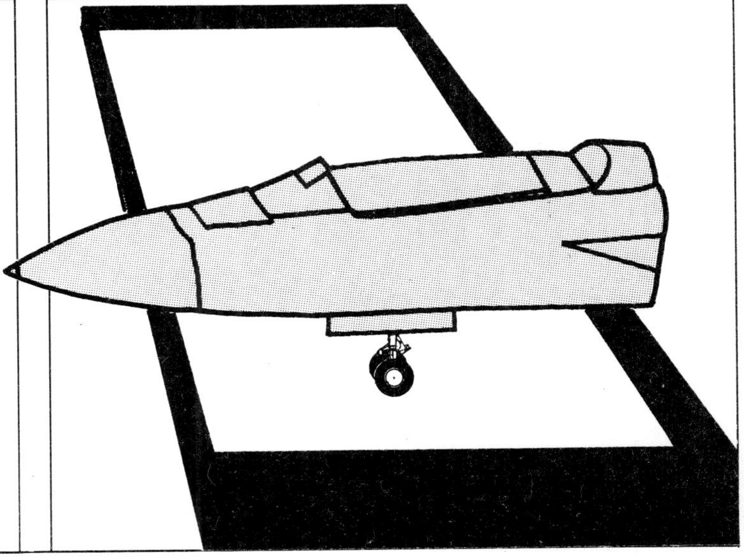

more work for you (ie, repairing joints that have separated because they were not fully 'cured') or completely ruin the whole kit. Whatever might happen, these possibilities can always be avoided by simply cultivating a little patience and by never rushing a model. If you find that you have spilled any liquid cement on your model (no matter how much) you would be best advised simply to leave it alone until it evaporates completely. Spilled tube cement is more difficult because it will burn any plastic it is allowed to sit on, so it should be removed quickly with a tissue. The plastic will be marked no matter what you do, but most damage of this sort can be put right by sanding the area with an abrasive once the cement has dried thoroughly. You may also find that when holding parts together with sticky tape the tape causes patches of glue to run from joints. Again, it is best simply to leave such areas until completely dry and then either file or sand the area clean. If you attempt to rectify any problems while the cement is wet you will only make matters much worse.

Aircraft cockpit canopies and fuselage windows, etc, are represented by clear plastic parts in kits, and although the clear plastic is essentially the same material as the rest in the kit box, rather more care has to be taken when cementing this material because even the smallest amount of cement will damage the clear plastic, which will lose the realistic 'see-through' effect. Consequently you must be careful to ensure that the cement only comes into contact with the edges of the part. The way to do this is to postion the piece (be it a window or canopy, or whatever) in its intended location as in a dry run, and then touch the edge of the joints with your liquid cement brush. The liquid cement will run along the joint line due to capillary action and with practice you will see how far the glue runs and where you need to re-apply cement. At all times you must be very careful not to apply too much cement otherwise it will ooze on to the clear areas. Some modellers choose to avoid using polystyrene cement on clear parts altogether and use PVA adhesive, the well-known 'white glue', which dries to a clear finish. It does not damage the clear plastic in any way and excess glue can be cleaned away with a damp cloth; however, it does not weld the plastic together as polystyrene cement does, and so the joint is not a very strong one. As a matter of personal choice you might prefer to use PVA glue rather than run the risks associated with normal cement.

If you do accidentally damage any clear parts, either with glue or by scratching, there is a way in which you can restore the part to a proper clear finish. Sand the damaged area with a very fine abrasive paper, using soapy water to enhance the fine polishing effect of the paper. Once the area is completely smooth you can polish the plastic with a metal polish. The precise type of polish you use does not really matter as all metal polishes are much the same. Buffing with a dry cloth will restore the clear finish and with patience the plastic will become completely restored. One thing you must avoid is to become heavy-handed with either the polishing or buffing, as undue pressure on the clear plastic will cause small stress lines to appear in the plastic, which will spoil the clear effect and cannot be removed. Even more pressure will break the plastic, so the rule is to perform all polishing in a slow and patient manner.

In cases where canopies or windows need to be cemented in an open position you will not be able to use PVA glue; polystyrene cement is a better alternative, although, whilst drying, the part will have to be held in an open position, either by tape or Plasticine. Because gravity will encourage parts such as these to fall towards a closed position, getting pieces to stay in the right place can be a problem. One solution is to use the famous 'superglue' (cyanoacrylate adhesive) which will fix any plastic part in position in a matter of seconds. There is no need to repeat here the dangers of using superglue in any circumstances, but extra care must be taken when sticking clear parts as superglue will damage a clear surface if

Above:
Seven $^1/_{48}$th scale A-4 Skyhawks, all built to an almost identical standard as a representation of the US Navy 'Blue Angels' aerobatic team. In the background is a huge $^1/_{48}$th scale Italeri C-130 which represents the support aircraft used by the team. Whilst much patience is needed to create a display such as this, some of the tedium can be relieved by building all the similar kits on a 'production- line' basis, rather than one at a time.

Below:
Canopies can be attached with PVA glue (which doesn't mark clear parts) or with polystyrene cement if used very carefully (it will cloud clear plastic). PVA can be applied thickly and the canopy placed on top, the excess glue being wiped away with a damp cloth. With polystyrene cement the canopy is fitted first and glue run along the joint line.

Glueing Canopies

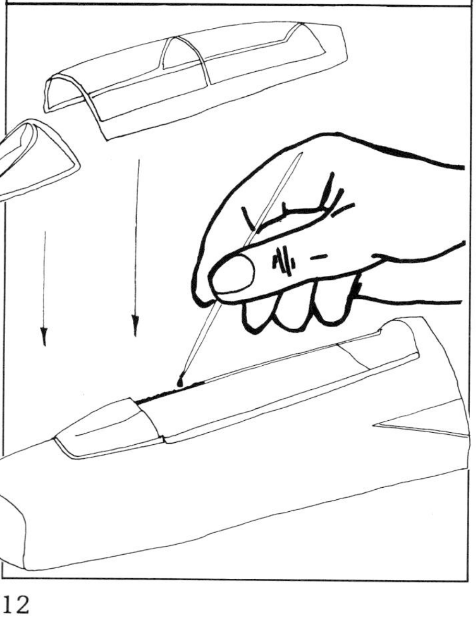

Below:
Abrasive 'wet and dry' paper will easily remove any surface blemishes and joint lines. Used wet, the paper will work even more effectively. Surface details will be lost, but can be re-scribed at a later stage.

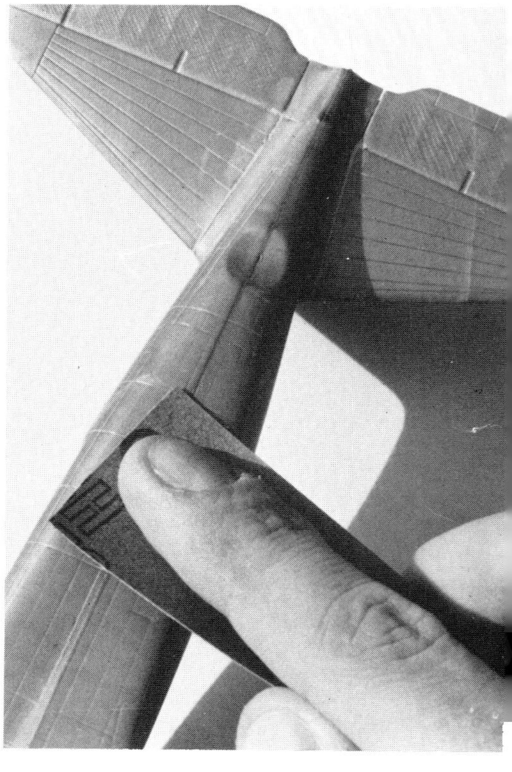

allowed to make contact. As with any glues, you must exercise great care in positioning the adhesive and never use too much.

Once the major parts have been properly joined and allowed to set fully you can set about cleaning up the many joints with abrasive paper, knife and file. Quite often you will come across places where there is a distinct gap between parts. Of course, real aircraft do not have great gaps or holes in their airframes, so in order to make a model as realistic as possible one has to attempt to remove all joint lines and gaps. This is done with a model filler. Fillers come in many forms, the most common plastic kit filler being a tube variety which is applied with a cocktail stick or similar and then allowed to set. Once dry the filler can be sanded and filed to the contours of the surrounding area. Like polystyrene cement the tube filler (or 'putty') will melt plastic, so you must avoid using too much filler at any one time. If an area needs much of the filler it is best to apply small amounts, allowing these to dry and then applying more filler on top rather than applying the whole lot at once. Sanding filler smooth is no great problem, although files and abrasive paper will clog with plastic and filler dust, so the most effective method of sanding is to use an abrasive paper dipped in water. For large gaps which would need quite large amounts of filler, a useful alternative to tube putty is the two-part epoxy putty (such as 'Milliput') which can be applied in one go, no matter how much you need. This filler comes as two lumps of putty which are mixed together in equal parts in whatever quantity is needed. Unlike the tube filler, this variety will dry at the same rate from inside and out so there is no need to apply small amounts in gradual steps. One small problem is that this filler does not keep as tight a grip on the plastic surface and can sometimes break away. To avoid this problem make sure that the plastic surface does not carry any greasy finger prints or dirt and try mixing a little liquid cement in with the putty, which will give it an extra 'bite'. Once dry the epoxy filler can be sanded in the normal way.

There are other types of fillers available, which are not directly aimed at model builders. Polyfiller can be used and is particularly easy to sand smooth, but it does tend to crumble when dry. For very small joint line gaps PVA glue is a useful filler which can be smoothed (while wet) with a damp cloth to the surrounding contours.

Once the gaps and large joint lines have been filled, they must be left for about 24 hours to dry properly. They can then be sanded smooth, as can any minor joint lines which did not need filling first. Although your instinct might be to rush on towards the painting stage, do not neglect the sanding process. Make completely sure that there are no gaps or joint lines and ridges. You will undoubtedly damage some of the moulded surface detail that is featured on most kits, but do not worry; this can all be easily re-scribed at a later stage. Use a fairly coarse abrasive paper initially to remove joints, filler and glue ridges, etc. Once they are all removed you can re-sand all the areas with a finer grade abrasive, used wet. When the basic airframe structure is acceptably smooth you can proceed towards adding the smaller parts such as tailplanes, undercarriage legs, underwing bomb racks or whatever.

Filling Gaps

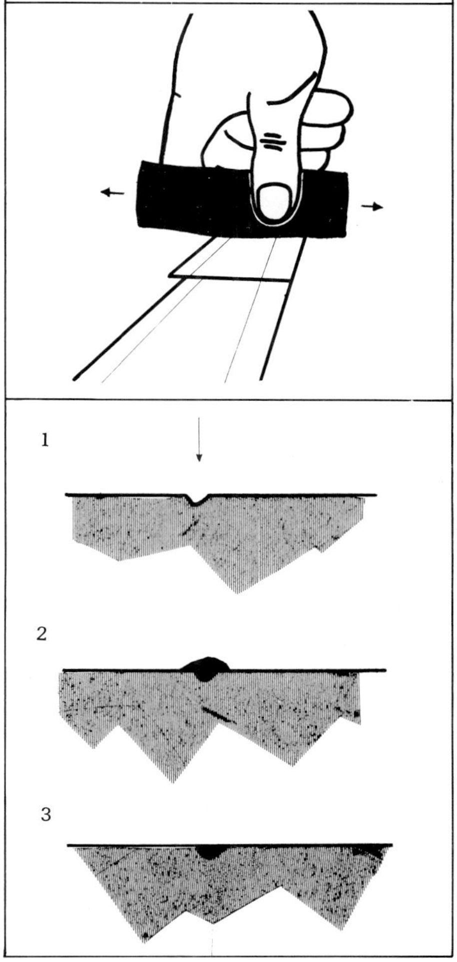

Above right:
Gaps or small trench-marks sometimes appear in odd places and need to be filled. A model filler should be applied to the area and, when dry, it can be sanded smooth. Never apply too much filler at once otherwise it might melt the plastic.

Below left:
Panel lines are often lost during the construction and sanding process. They can easily be restored with a scalpel and metal ruler.

Below right:
Application of filler will remove any gaps or cracks in a model's surface. Once dry, the filler can be sanded smooth to match the surrounding contours. Filler application can be messy, but a surrounding mask of sticky tape will keep the filler to the desired places.

Re-Scribing Panel Lines

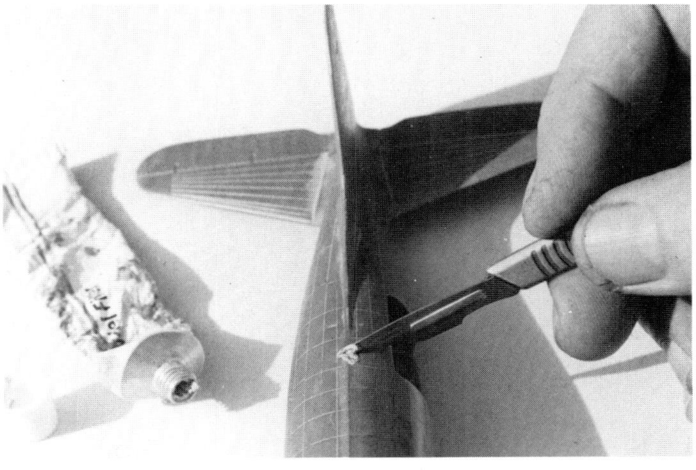

Double trouble

Those with a passion for aircraft of the older variety will have some particular construction problems that are peculiar to the world of biplanes. Such elderly aircraft are often looked upon as 'double trouble' with two (or even three) sets of wings, all of which have to be assembled neatly and correctly. Nevertheless, the construction of biplane models can be a very rewarding experience and the end result is always well worth the effort. Like any other kit the main part of the airframe will be the fuselage, which can be constructed and detailed in the normal manner. The wings require a slightly different approach. The lower of the two sets of wings will normally be attached directly to the fuselage, and so it is a simple task to assemble these pieces in the usual way. The second and upper wing assembly is not directly connected to the fuselage, however, and the most common arrangement is for the upper wings to be attached to the lower wings and fuselage by a series of interplane struts and rigging wires. Once the lower wings have been fitted to the fuselage, the various interplane struts should be cemented to the lower wing. Of course they should all stand upright, although not necessarily vertically because they can quite often be raked forwards or backwards — check the instructions. To keep the struts in an upright position, Plasticine can be used to hold the pieces in place until dry. Superglue would make this task much easier (because of the speedy drying time) but polystyrene cement is preferable because the struts will all have corresponding holes in the upper wing to which they will eventually be secured, and it is safe to assume that the struts will need slight readjustments to their positions to allow them to fit into their respective holes. Superglue will not allow any small movements to be made, whereas liquid cement will. Once the struts are cemented in place, the upper wing can be attached to the tops of the struts. This can be a time-consuming job, as the struts will all need to be coaxed into their locating holes with the aid of tweezers. Certainly it would be very unwise to rush this job. Once all the struts have been correctly routed to their holes, and the joints have been cemented, the whole assembly must be left to dry completely. The upper wing will probably move around on its flimsy supports, so care must be taken to ensure that the upper wing is allowed to set in a straight position in relation to the lower wing and fuselage. Make sure that the upper wing is precisely parallel to the lower. Once you are sure of its position, find a place where the whole assembly can be left to set dry. The wings can be held in place by nudging the wing tips with a book or paint tin, just sufficiently to prevent the upper wing from slowly slipping out of line whilst drying. Once the model is safely wedged between supporting books, etc, it should be left for at least a day.

Below:
This illustration from the Matchbox Tiger Moth instruction sheet shows how the upper wing of a biplane usually sits on the top of supporting struts. What the instructions don't show, however, is that the struts must be cemented firmly to the lower halves before the upper wing is attached. Never attach the struts to both wings at the same time, as this will result in an uncontrollable disaster!

Assembling Biplane Wings

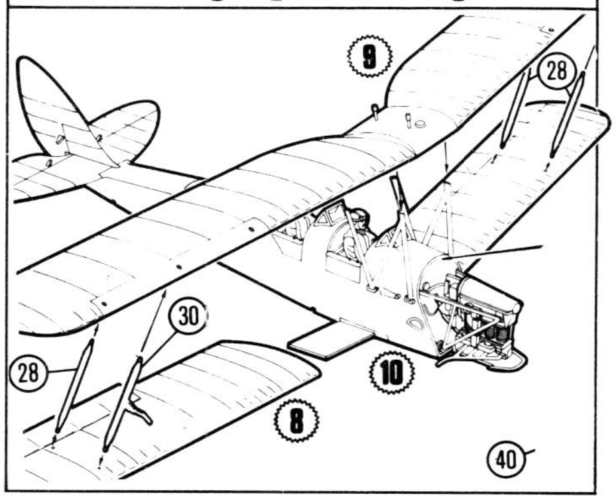

Below:
The Airfix Avro 504 (left) and the Revell SE5A make an interesting duo and a good comparison with a pair of modern fighters.

When painting biplanes, there are a few difficulties that will be encountered. Firstly, once the model is assembled, the struts and wires between the wings will make painting a very difficult task, especially if you have to camouflage the upper surface of the lower wing, for example . . . imagine getting your paintbrush between those wires! Of course, the only sensible thing to do is to paint the wings before assembly. Because the lower wings can be attached to the fuselage before painting, only the upper wings will be separate from the aircraft when you apply the paint, thus there will not be any further joint lines to remove at any stage; and in any case there is no reason why you should not paint the wings at this stage. As all the constructional work will have been completed, there should not be any reason why the painted surfaces should suffer any further damage. You should also take into account the application of transfers. Quite often the wing roundels, crosses or other markings have interplane struts that sit directly on top of them. Obviously you really cannot apply a decal on to a wing when there is a strut in the way, so you must apply the wing markings before attaching the struts. These common-sense rules are not difficult to follow, but reflect the need for a good deal of forward-thinking when building biplanes.

Once the wings have been allowed to dry firmly, the airframe assembly should be essentially complete. There remains one additional task that will really enhance the model, this being the addition of rigging wires. Both the wings and tailplane will feature a number of bracing wires, their precise location being dependent on the aircraft type, but it is rare for kit instructions to even mention the location of the rigging, and the box top painting is sometimes the only guide. Of course, the ever-important photograph is almost essential to give a full picture of which wire goes where. Representing rigging wires on a model can be done in many ways. The bracing wire must be as thin as possible, in order to look anything like a scaled-down version of the real wire. String is useless because it is far too thick and breaks into tiny strands; nylon wire is a better alternative, especially the thin fishing line variety. Stretched plastic sprue is also useful, but it is easily broken. Human hair is perhaps the best material as it is of the correct thickness, it is quite strong and it costs nothing! Quite how you attach the rigging is a matter of personal choice. It can be glued to the upper and lower wings, although extreme care must be taken to avoid great lumps of glue forming at the ends of the rigging where it is attached to the wing. Also you have to get the wire to the precise length before cementing it in place, but a pair of compass dividers will allow you to do this quite effectively. PVA white glue is the best adhesive for the job. The main problem with attaching rigging in this manner is that it can sometimes sag after a period of time and thus it loses its realistic effect (it is supposed to be stretched tight!). As a result you might have to spend quite a lot of time continually replacing sagged rigging.

A much more effective way of attaching rigging is to drill very small holes in the wings at the location point. The rigging wire can then be fed through the hole, cemented in place and the end of the wire cut flush with the wing when dry. Obviously this means that the location holes will have to be re-sealed and painted over, but the end result is generally more effective. Some larger sized biplane kits have the individual wings divided into upper and lower halves that have to be cemented together. In this case only the inner faces of the wings need be drilled with rigging holes and nylon wire can be fed through each hole in turn, all, in one piece, before the wing halves are cemented together. After the assembly is completed, the rigging can be pulled tight and 'anchored' in just one place. This means that the rigging is kept tight at all times, as the 'wires' are in fact just one wire which runs through the small space between the wing halves. However, on smaller kits that have wings moulded as one-piece structures this approach cannot be employed.

Stretching Sprue

Above:
Stretching 'sprue' (the plastic runner frame that surrounds the kit parts) is a useful pastime. Depending on the thickness you stretch to, the strands of plastic can be used for a whole range of subjects. Any piece of sprue can be used, and all one has to do is gently warm the piece over a flame (a gas cooker is the most effective) and turn the plastic whilst it heats. When it begins to swell and twist in the middle, move it away from the heat and slowly pull the ends apart. Note that the plastic should not be burned otherwise it will give off poisonous fumes.

Assembling Biplane Wings

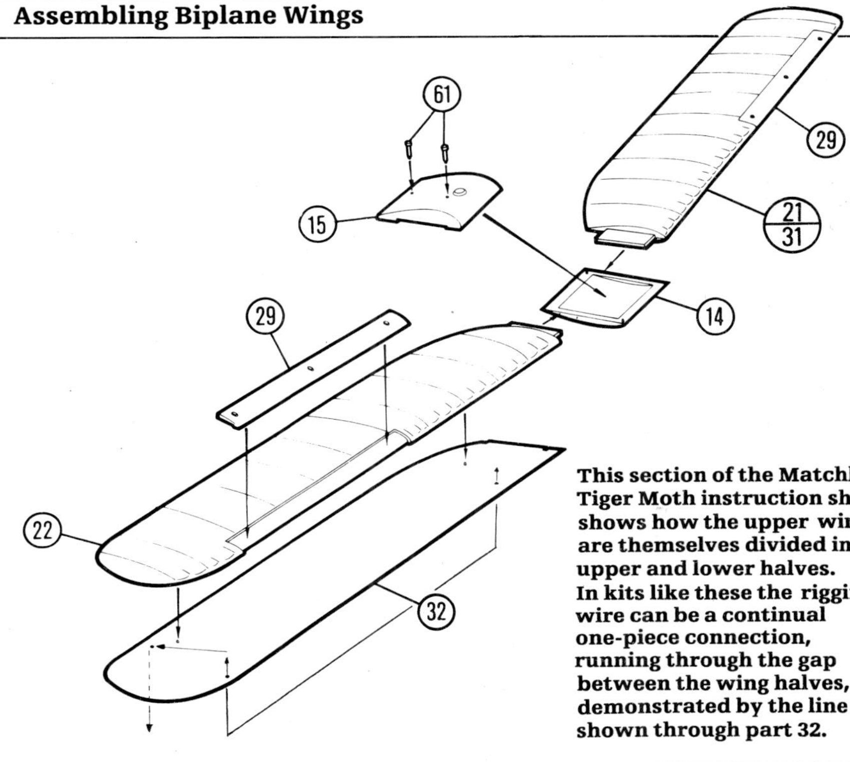

This section of the Matchbox Tiger Moth instruction sheet shows how the upper wings are themselves divided into upper and lower halves.
In kits like these the rigging wire can be a continual one-piece connection, running through the gap between the wing halves, as demonstrated by the line shown through part 32.

A touch of colour

Painting is often the most rewarding stage of modelling as it is the point where a box of plastic finally starts to take on the appearance of an authentic replica. Unfortunately painting can also be one of the most frustrating parts of the hobby and is the downfall of many a good model. However, with care and the all-important patience, painting can become a straightforward and pleasurable process. When all the sanding is complete and the model is smooth from joints, etc, it should be given a thorough wash in order to remove all traces of dust and dirt. Because of the plastic manufacturing process the kit parts will probably have traces of grease on them, which should also be removed during the washing stage. A little detergent in the water will help this. If you have attached any small detail parts you must be careful to avoid damaging or breaking them whilst washing. Of course, before attempting to wash the model, with experience you will learn just what can be attached to the kit and what cannot. Once clean, the whole assembly should be left to dry naturally. Never use tissues to assist the drying, as this will simply result in masses of dust and paper particles that will stick to the surfaces. Using a hair dryer or heater of any sort to speed up the drying will probably melt and warp the plastic, so there is no real alternative to simply sitting back and waiting again!

When you are satisfied that all water has evaporated, you can then turn your attention to applying paint. In almost every instance one can imagine a better end result will be achieved if you first apply an undercoat of matt white paint. Apart from providing a base of uniform colour on which to apply the colours, the undercoat will also serve to highlight any marks and blemishes which you may have missed during the sanding process. Quite often small marks are not noticed until paint is applied, and the white paint will easily indicate any places where further minor sanding might be necessary. If you do come across any such places you should wait until the undercoat is completely dry and then sand the area smooth in the normal way. The dust can then be carefully removed with a brush (the photographic lens brushes are the most effective) and a coat of white can be applied. The undercoat really needs to be only a thin layer of paint, so if you apply the paint with a brush you should make sure that the paint is of a fairly thin consistency, which can be achieved by adding a little thinning agent to the paint. A quicker and more convenient approach (albeit a more expensive one) is to purchase a spray can of matt white paint. This can be quickly applied with the minimum of fuss and will not be too thick. If you are fortunate enough to own a hobby air brush, applying an undercoat should be a very easy affair. If any clear parts

Below:
Hand-painting requires practice. A straight-edged brush might be an advantage, but the simple rule to follow, is to keep the paint brush flowing in one direction, gradually working along the surface. Never try to apply a thick coat or disaster is guaranteed! Let the first coat dry thoroughly; if it is too thin, apply a second coat later.

Hand Painting

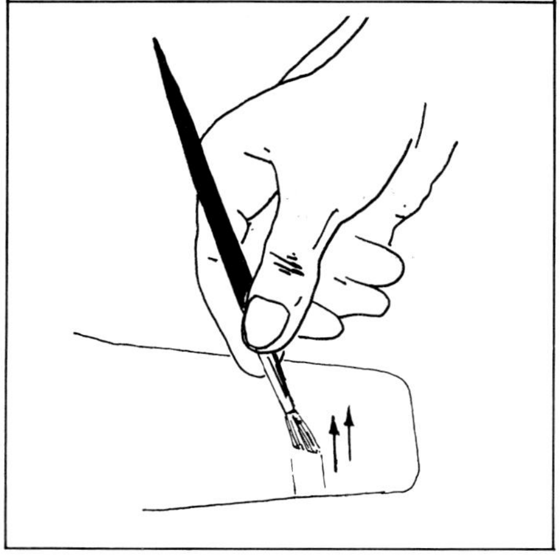

Above:
The range of model paints expands regularly, although there are only two basic types of paint, these being oil-based enamel, and acrylic which is water based. Another useful bottled solution is Microscale's 'Krystal Kleer' which can be used instead of clear plastic to fill small window apertures. PVA white glue has a similar function.

(windows, etc) have already been attached to the model you will have to cover these areas before painting to avoid them becoming coated with paint. The simplest way is to use sticky tape which can be laid over the clear part and carefully cut to the shape of the clear area, the surrounding excess tape being pulled away. Another way is to brush-paint on to a quick-drying masking fluid (available at all hobby shops). After painting, the masking fluid (which will dry to a rubbery finish) can be peeled away to reveal the clear plastic beneath.

Once you have achieved a completely uniform white undercoat over the entire model you are almost ready to apply the first colours. Before this stage you might wish to smooth the surface of the kit still further by lightly sanding the undercoat with a very fine abrasive paper, although this is by no means necessary in every instance. Having established that all traces of dust are removed from the kit, you are ready to paint. Because all modelling paints are fairly thin in consistency there is no easy way in which lighter colours (white, yellow, red, etc) can be applied over darker colours, so you must always remember that the colours should be applied in sequence, starting with the lightest and working towards the darkest as the final colour.

There are two types of paint which can be used on plastic models. Enamel is by far the most popular (the Humbrol range being the most famous) and is widely available in many shops. It can be brush-painted directly from the tin, although to make the paint less thick (which is often desirable) enamel thinners should be stirred into the paint in small amounts. A fairly recent development is the arrival of acrylic paints, water-based (as opposed to oil-based) colours that can be thinned with warm water. They will work just as effectively as enamels and the thinner will cost you nothing! However, it does dry very rapidly, which can cause problems with brush-painting, and you will still have to purchase an acrylic thinner to wash your paint brushes. It does not really matter which type you use as long as you stick either to one or the other. Only the most experienced modellers manage to successfully use both types on one model!

Paints are also sold in the two basic types of either matt or gloss. Initially you are best advised to stick to matt colours, as they will dry faster and are often easier to apply. If the colour scheme on the instruction sheet suggests a gloss finish you can easily apply a clear varnish after the painting is complete. The paint should be thoroughly mixed before use, as the paint pigment and the oil in which it is suspended easily become separated. If you do not mix regularly the paint will not dry at all. To mix the paint a good hard shake of the tin will help, but the better method is to thoroughly stir the contents with the end of a small screwdriver or matchstick, etc. Always make sure the paint is stirred for longer than you think necessary, as this is the only sure way of fully mixing the contents.

The painting brush you use should be fairly small and of the typical hobby type which can be bought at any model shop. Before dipping it into the paint you should check whether there are any loose bristles because you do not want to drop hairs into the paint or on to the model. If you can afford to spend a pound or so on a brush, you should buy a high-quality artist's brush from an

Above:
An air brush is an expensive item that was once considered a luxury. Now many modellers have an airbrush, which will give a smooth paint finish free of brush marks. More importantly, careful work will allow soft edge sprayed camouflage to be achieved.

Convenient Painting

Attaching your model to a stick or hanging it from nylon string are just two ways of keeping the model off your fingers while painting it.

Painting Small Parts

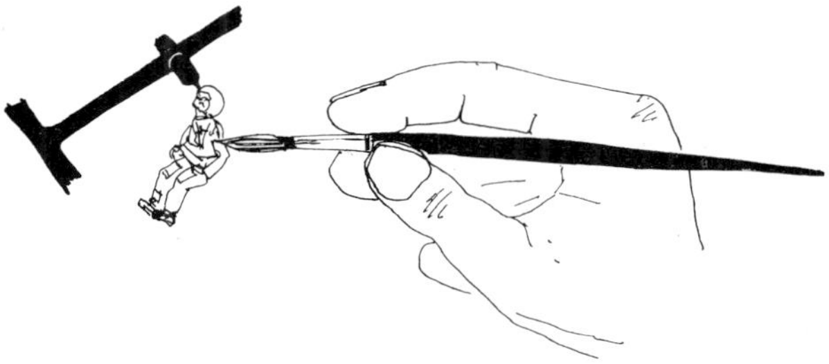

Smaller parts can often be painted whilst still attached to the sprue, thus saving a lot of fiddly work later on.

Masking

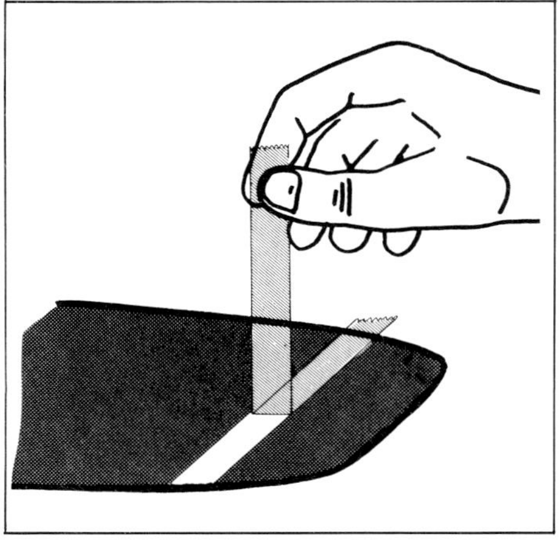

Masking Camouflage Edges

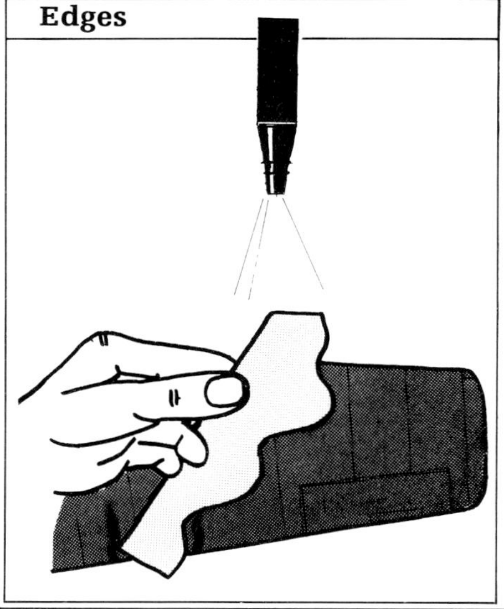

Left:
Any paint colour can be protected from coverage by more paint by applying masking tape or fluid. For fairly flat surfaces where tape can adhere, masking tape or household sticky tape will do the job, but for complicated curved areas a masking fluid should be painted on and allowed to dry. Both tape and fluid masking can be peeled away after the painting is complete. Tape should be pulled across the surface rather than directly upwards, as the latter may cause the painted surface to be pulled from the model with the tape.

A Matchbox Hurricane, revealing an effective soft-edge camouflage scheme achieved by careful use of an airbrush.

Left:
Those who cannot achieve a satisfactory soft edge by using an airbrush 'by hand' should use a card mask held just above the model surface.

art shop. It will give you a consistently better result and will last you a long time providing it is cleaned well after each use.

The actual process of applying the paint to the model surface is a stage that improves with practice. You might like to try painting some scraps of plastic first, to become familiar with the process, but in reality there's little to it. Remember not to overload the brush with paint (only a small amount at a time) and to take time in applying the colour. If you find that the paint begins to thicken or even dry while you're still painting, it is too thick and should be thinned slightly with a drop of enamel (or acrylic, if it is acrylic paint!) thinner. If the paint appears too thin (ie, you can see streaks of the undercoat beneath) simply carry on and finish the job. When the paint is dry you can add another coat. What you should never do is apply a thick coat in one go or add a second coat while the first is still wet. These actions will lead to disaster! Like every other stage in modelling, there's no substitute for waiting.

After only a little practice you'll acquire the right approach to painting. Try to use long flowing strokes of the brush rather than a series of dabs, and always stroke the brush in the same direction — for example, you should ideally paint a wing with a series of strokes from the leading to trailing edges. If you find that the brush is becoming loaded with paint, stop painting and wash the brush in thinners, then carry on. Like glues, there is no set time in which a paint will dry: much depends on the temperature and humidity, but the main factor is the particular type or brand of paint. Most will be dry to the touch in an hour or so, especially matt finishes which often dry in minutes; however, all paints take much longer to dry than you would first imagine. Do not be fooled into thinking that the paint is dry even if it feels so. Regardless of its appearance you really need to allow an overnight period for a coat to dry thoroughly, and even longer if you intend to apply another coat on top, otherwise the first colour will simply pull off when the second is applied. Yet again, you need patience!

Once the paint is fully dried, you can check for any blemishes in the finish. If there are none you can proceed to the next colour, but if there are some you should return to the fine abrasive paper and lightly sand the affected area, and then repaint it.

One of the most important aspects of brush-painting is the care of the brushes. They must be kept completely clean of paint and should be rinsed thoroughly in thinners after use, otherwise they will be useless after the first painting session. Oil-based enamels (rinsed in enamel thinners) can be rinsed in Polyclense and then washed in warm water to achieve a fully clean finish. Acrylics should be rinsed well in acrylic thinners, then in hot water.

Many modellers find that they can achieve much more effective results with spray paints, which come in aerosol spray cans. You must be careful to purchase the correct type of paint however, as the modeller's enamel spray is sold in a can which looks outwardly similar to car lacquer spray. Of course, the latter is not what the modeller is looking for and will seriously damage the surface of a plastic model, so check at the time of purchase that you have the right type of paint. The use of a spray can is very simple, as the can only has to be given a thorough shake, and the paint can then be sprayed on to the model. The paint flows very quickly from the can, so you have to keep the spray moving over the model or you'll find a pool of paint forming at any place where the paint spray lingers. As with brush-painting you must resist the temptation to apply too much paint at once in an effort to achieve a solid coat of colour. If you spray too much at once the paint will run all over the place, so the practice of applying successive thin coats is the only wise approach. One definite advantage of a spray finish is that the coat will dry much quicker and thus a second coat can be applied in only a couple of hours. The chief advantage is that there are no brush marks to contend with, leaving the brush-painting for the delicate detailed parts such as wheels, etc. One disadvantage of spray cans is that they are very expensive in relation to the amount of paint each can produces. They also spray a very wide area at any given time, so there's no way you could spray a camouflage colour over a different shade, for example, without masking the first coat; the paint spray would cover everything.

To achieve a spray finish that can be directed at specific places you need an air brush. Such tools are very expensive (around £50) and are not the kind of investment the first-time modeller should consider, but if you're eager to improve your models and you're not satisfied with the paint finish, the air brush becomes an essential. The air brush is a pen-shaped tool which sprays a fine jet of compressed air, into which a small amount of paint is introduced. Through a fully variable control setting you can alter the amount of air or paint in any combination you need to achieve, either a wide spray of paint like a spray can or just a thin line of colour, rather like the flow from a pen. Of course, the latter is ideal for spraying colours such as two-tone camouflage where one colour has a 'soft' edge. (This is because the full-size machines are painted with spray guns, of which the air brush is a miniature version.) Like any brush, air brushes have to be kept very clean and completely free from any traces of paint when not in use. This involves an often messy procedure of rinsing with thinners and the regular dismantling of the tool, which can make air brushing very tedious. Nevertheless the results which can be achieved with an air brush are truly astonishing, and any serious modeller would be advised to consider the purchase of one.

Painting Soft Camouflage Edges

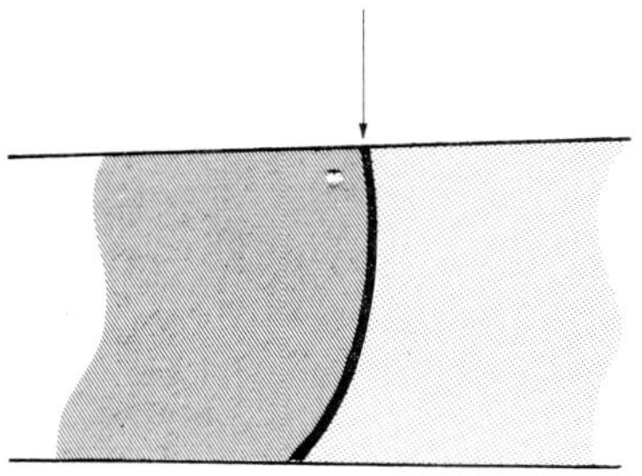

To obtain a good representation of a soft camouflage edge, using only paint brushes, a 50/50 mix of the camouflage colours can be painted on to the model to leave a thin line of the mix between the camouflage colours. Even with fairly close inspection the effect will look like a soft sprayed edge. However, the blending line must be very thin.

The art of air brushing is one which must be learned through constant practice, and the more time one spends painting scraps of plastic, the better the eventual results. Much depends on the thickness of the paint which is contained in the air brush paint cup. All paints must be thinned quite considerably in air brushes in order to prevent the nozzle blocking, but the precise amount depends on the type of brush and personal experience. Fairly thick paint will spray an even coat over a fairly large area, whereas a thin paint will spray fine edges. As with spray cans the paint must flow over the model in a sweeping motion because the paint will gather into pools and run if the spray stays in one place for too long. You will find that even after practice you have to experiment with the thickness of each paint you use on every occasion before applying any to the model. Never spray directly on to a model with a fresh supply of paint, as almost inevitably the first drops of colour will splatter out from the brush in all directions. Always start the application of each colour on a scrap of plastic and become completely satisfied with the paint flow before attempting to touch the model. After becoming familiar with the use of a good quality air brush you'll find that endless effects can be achieved, and the use of a normal paint brush will be restricted to the painting of smaller detailed parts. One point to remember is that many manufacturers sell very inexpensive air brush sets for just a few pounds. In practice these are little more than spray guns, offering no variety of spray finish. They might be very useful for painting one uniform colour over a large area, but they will not allow you to perform any of the possibilities that are open to a high quality air brush. The basic rule is that the more expensive the air brush, the better its results (with practice!).

The flow of compressed air in the brush comes from one of two sources. Beginners often use an aerosol can of compressed air. These are very effective but only supply a limited amount of air for a fairly high cost. Regular modellers always use an electric air compressor. These are even more expensive than the air brush and can cost between £50 and £100. Although the initial outlay is high, they will supply an endless flow of air at a fairly low cost for the electricity supply. If you intend sticking with the modelling hobby, a compressor is an essential addition to your air brush.

One aspect of modelling which is especially appropriate to air brushing is that of masking. Although you will have probably had to mask the clear canopy or windows before applying paint of any sort, spraying paint is rather less predictable than a hand brush, and all areas that do not require covering in any given colour must be masked by some method, otherwise spots of paint will inevitably stray on to the surface. When applying coats of colour (the darker) over other shades (the lighter), the first colour will have to be masked unless you are capable of carefully spraying the second colour in thin lines (this only applies to camouflage effects). For shades which have a distinct sharp line the first colour will need to be masked with tape to give the sharp, straight line to which the next colour can be painted. Having made sure that the first colour is completely dry, sticky tape is still likely to pull paint from the model surface when removed, so it must be made less tacky by rubbing the sticky side with your fingers. Alternatively you can use masking tape which is specifically manufactured for this purpose, and is consequently less tacky, or masking fluid which can be painted on and then peeled off after use. Whether you use tape or fluid is really a matter of personal choice, and experience will tell you which type is the more convenient for you.

To summarise, whatever type of painting you use, the end result can always be successful providing you do not rush the procedure. Make sure that every coat of paint is left to dry completely. If you make any mistakes, such as painting the wrong area or dropping spots of paint in the wrong place, do not try and repair the damage while the paint is still wet. In every instance all such problems can be rectified by sanding away the paint with fine abrasive paper and repainting, but the surface must be completely dry before you attempt anything.

What colour?

This is a question that is often asked by many modellers, and one to which there is often a whole variety of answers. Unfortunately no aircraft is simply painted in one perfect coat of colour, as there is no such thing. Even if there was such an aircraft, representing even one colour on a model opens up a range of questions that need to be asked. One important point is that if you paint a model aircraft in exactly the same colour as its full-sized counterpart, the model will look wrong. This is because you have to appreciate how a model is regarded by an observer. A $^{1}/_{72}$nd scale model seen from just a few feet away is rather like looking at a real aircraft from perhaps a hundred feet or more away, such is the relative scale distance. Given that this is the case, imagine looking at a grey/green camouflaged aircraft from a hundred feet away. Do you see two vivid camouflage colours? No, of course you don't, in fact the further away from the object you are, the more it tends to take on a uniform grey appearance, and it is worth bearing this in mind when painting a model. Another considerable colour effect is caused by the light conditions under which you view the aircraft. A grey/green camouflage might look like two shades of grey, almost identical in tone, on a dark and rainy day. Look again on a bright sunny day and you see two distinct contrasting colours. Look at the camouflage on a matt-finished aircraft compared to a gloss-finished machine, and just marvel at the difference a coat of gloss varnish can make to colour.

Colour is indeed a very complicated subject, and any modeller is therefore advised to become well acquainted with the effects of colour. To take an example, the RAF training aircraft fleet carries a standard red, white and grey colour scheme and for modellers of Hawks, Jet Provosts and so on it is important to obtain the correct paint matches for the colour scheme. Unfortunately most kit instructions do not give much detail as to what precise paint colours are needed for each aircraft (although, thankfully, things are now improving in this aspect) and many modellers identify the RAF Support Command Red as being simply a bright red and nothing more. After visiting the local model shop, many inevitably return home with a 'Bright Red'. Sadly, the latter colour is often more correctly identified as Post Office Red, as opposed to the Signal Red which is used on the real aircraft. As a result there are many models of RAF training aircraft that appear to be painted in a sort of cherry-coloured red that is far darker than the correct colour. This is a relatively simple example, but there are many others. If you cannot be completely sure as to what constitutes a bright red, you can only imagine things such as the three shades of light grey used on a RAF Phantom, for example!

The only way to become completely familiar with the vast range of colours used on modern and older aircraft alike is to identify paint reference numbers. All colours are identified in British Standard references and in the American Federal Standard reference system. At long last, kit instruction sheets are starting to give colour references that give either a British (BS. . .) or American (FS. . .) code number that can be matched to an actual tin of paint, so there is no chance of confusion any more. Even the kits which do not give references can easily be checked in commercial model magazines, which regularly give such colour

Below left:
The Harvard has been seen in endless colour schemes, but for a unique model the Korean aquatic version is an eye-catcher!

Below right:
Airfix's Spitfire VB, displaying a very effective sprayed edge camouflage and weathered paintwork.

scheme details. However, there are always exceptions to the rule and it is beneficial to have at least some idea as to the effects of mixing paints. For example, you might already know that you can mix a blue paint with a yellow paint to obtain a green and a red/yellow mix will give an orange. A red/blue mix will become purple, a red/white mix produces pink, black and white mixes to a grey and a blue/orange mix will give a brown. These are just basic facts, but as you can imagine, the precise shades you get depend on the shades of colours you choose to mix.

In fact there is an endless range of colours which can be found by mixing other colours together, and the only way you will ever find them is by experimentation. This is recommended practice that is very informative and great fun! Neither is it a particularly messy affair, nor expensive, as you only need a spot of two colours to make another, and you can always scale-up the proportions at a later stage if you wish to make a quantity of any given colour. A sheet of white plastic card is an ideal surface on which to dabble, with the aid of a mixing tool (cocktail sticks are cheapest) and a standby supply of tissue to clean up any mess (good old toilet roll is easily the cheapest and most effective!). Take some of your paint tins and drop a spot of each colour on to your white surface and have a thorough dabble with the various colours that can be made. Try applying white too, which will give you a good idea of how basic shades can be changed quite effectively. Once you have become familiar with the effects the mixing of colours can have, you will soon find that you can analyse even shades of grey and determine exactly how to reproduce such shades on your model. Many people are apprehensive of mixing colours because of their fear of mess and expense. Providing you are

Above and top:
The smooth paint finish on this Monogram 1/48th AH-1S Cobra would benefit from a little weathering. *Monogram*

Below:
Monogram's 1/48th scale AH-64 Apache. Note that the main rotor blades droop slightly towards their tips, as on a real helicopter. The kit parts will invariably be straight, and it is up to the modeller to add the final touch of realism by (carefully) incorporating a slight droop to the blades. *Monogram*

willing to try small-scale experiments first, you can save yourself any mess and a lot of money before mixing large quantities of colour.

An eye for colour is essential, as no matter how many paints are produced there will never be a tin of paint to match every colour you will need. Do not forget to take into account lighting conditions when you are applying or mixing colours. If you mix your paints at night under a household lamp, you find that you have a completely different colour in the light of day. This is because normal daylight is essentially a blue-white light, as opposed to the common light bulb which gives out an orange-coloured light. Remember too that if you have to match colours to a photograph, the photographic reproduction may have slightly altered the colours and a whole range of photographs of the same subject will give you a much better 'average' idea of the colour you are looking at. Also remember that even in sunlight a colour will differ depending on the time of day an aircraft is seen. At midday the sun is high, in a clear sky, whereas at dawn or evening the sun hits the object from low down, maybe through an orange haze.

If you intend to apply a gloss varnish to your model after painting, remember that varnish will alter the contrast of the colours dramatically. A gloss finish will increase the contrast, whilst a matt varnish will have an opposite effect. Another point is that a paint undercoat will affect the top coat shade. If the kit plastic is red and you apply white, for example, you will see what happens: pink! As a rule, it is wise to apply a white undercoat on to which the surface colours have a neutral base. This is especially important if you are applying reds, yellows, oranges, etc, that are not particularly opaque and easily show an undercoat colour if there is one. The most famous example is dayglow orange, which is a very peculiar colour and almost transparent in quality. If you attempt to apply this over grey, black or any coloured plastic you will forever keep applying coats without achieving the end shade! In this case, there is a very obvious need for a base undercoat of white.

There are so many facets of colour applications that space precludes a complete exploration of the subject. The simple fact is that you cannot take colours for granted, and the more you can learn about colour effect, so much the better.

Below:
A Curtiss Seagull (Hasegawa) to the right, the Monogram F4B4 to the left, with a Monogram Goshawk to the rear. This is a fascinating trio of tiny $^{1}/_{72}$nd scale models, all built to a high standard.

Bottom left:
The Esci/Italeri C-47 can be altered or painted to represent literally hundreds of different Dakota variants. Here is a former TV star from Yorkshire Television's *Airline* series, built with the aid of scratch-made markings. The small display base adds to the overall effect.

Bottom right:
Hasegawa's Nakajima 'Rita' is something slightly out of the ordinary, in an overall orange colour scheme.

Another touch of colour

Whilst painting is a major stage in the transformation of a model from just an assembly of plastic parts to a scale replica, there are further steps needed to complete the task, these being the application of insignia and other small markings as well as the addition of weathering effects. With any kit you will find that although the overall colour scheme is normally applied by paint, smaller areas of colour, especially unit markings and national insignia, are printed as a decal (or 'transfer') sheet. Decal sheets are simple to use, the basic method being to soak the sheet in water which will allow the printed markings to become detached from their paper backing sheet. Each item can then be placed on to the model and left to dry. Although the method of applying decals could not be more simple, the careless use of decals can easily spoil a model, reducing the overall effect to nothing more than a toy. With a more careful and thoughtful application, a set of decal sheet markings can enhance the authenticity and attractiveness of a model.

Once the painting of your model is complete, you must consider the final finish of the surface, which will either be gloss or matt (or possibly both) depending on which type of paint you have used. In most cases the surface will be matt, which means that the whole model needs to be painted with a gloss varnish, either by brush or spray. You may well have read from the kit instruction sheet that the final finish should be matt, and indeed most military aircraft do have a matt surface, but the reason for applying a gloss varnish is to aid the decals in becoming secured properly to the model's surface. You will find that if you attempt to fix any decals to a matt paint they will not properly adhere to the surface and will either break away if touched or leave patches of a cloudy, silvering effect, known as decal film. The reason for this is simple: the decal is a series of printed inks suspended in a layer of varnish, which lies on top of the paint surface. If the finish is gloss, the decal can lay flat and fit snugly on to the paint; however, if the paint is matt, the paint surface will be full of microscopic ridges and lumps which will leave small pockets of air between the decal and the paint surface. Consequently, the decal cannot adhere to the paint. Applying a gloss varnish ensures that the decal has a uniform smooth coat on to which it can lay. Of course, once the decals have all been applied, the model can be repainted or sprayed with whatever surface sheen you desire, by applying the appropriate varnish.

Apart from odd exceptions, full-size aircraft do not carry any markings in decal form, relying instead on careful hand painting aided by stencils. On a model it is rarely possible to make stencils small enough to directly paint markings, so we have to use decals. Even so, we can take steps to ensure that the decal takes on the appearance of a painted marking. The first step is described above, but there are others too. For each individual marking you should cut carefully around the colours

Below:
Applying decals can be a tricky business, but providing care and patience is exercised there should be no problems. A sharp pair of scissors, tweezers and decal setting solution will add to the likelihood of successful application.
Ron Firth/Pamag Publications

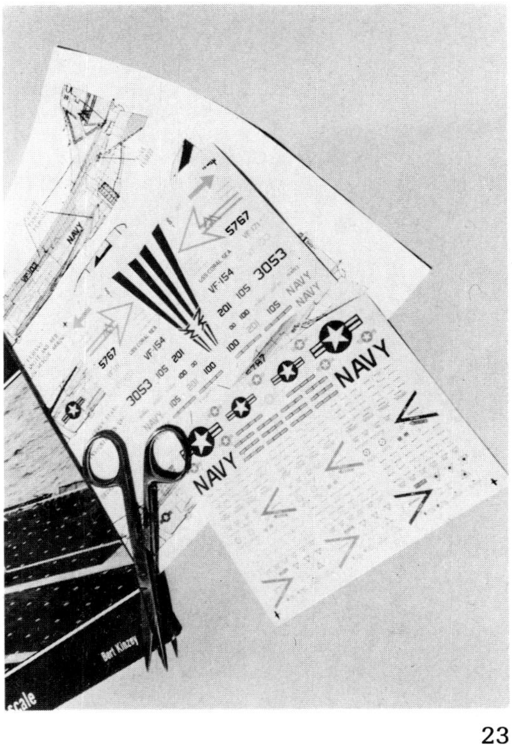

Top:
A unit with a distinguished history, No 111 (Treble-One) Squadron gained fame as an aerobatic team known as the Black Arrows. It is now equipped with Phantom FG1s, flying from RAF Leuchars in the air defence role. XV574 'Z-Zulu', flagship of the fleet and the Squadron Commander's aircraft, here carries the traditional colours of the squadron.

Centre:
The F-15C Eagle illustrated is an aircraft of the 53rd TFS at Bitburg AB, and is depicted armed with four AIM-7M Sparrows, AIM-9M Sidewinders and a 20mm cannon.

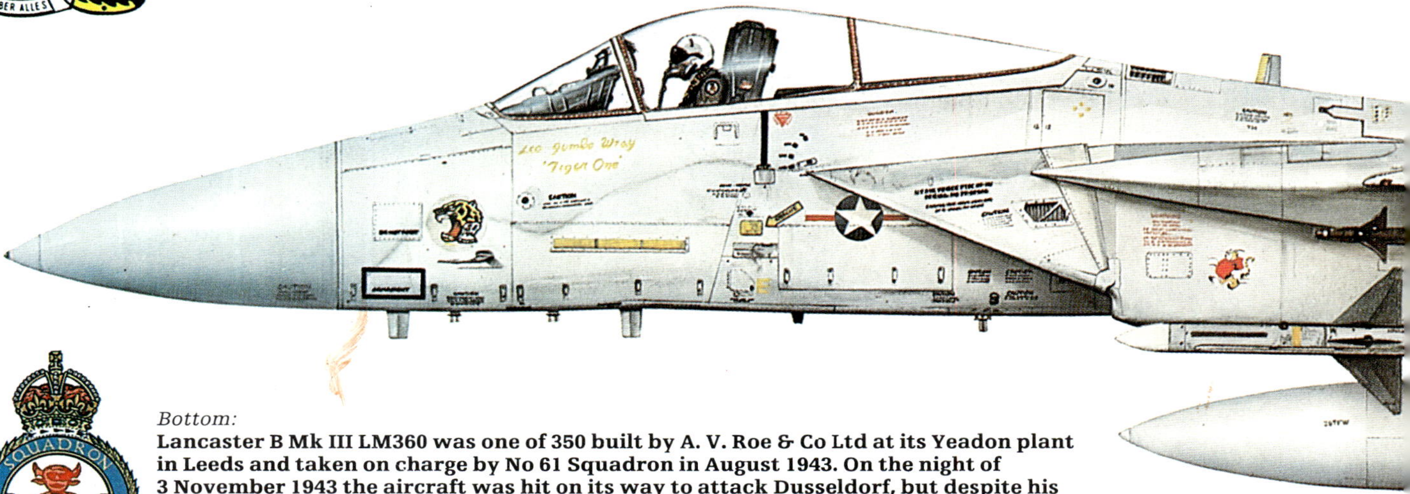

Bottom:
Lancaster B Mk III LM360 was one of 350 built by A. V. Roe & Co Ltd at its Yeadon plant in Leeds and taken on charge by No 61 Squadron in August 1943. On the night of 3 November 1943 the aircraft was hit on its way to attack Dusseldorf, but despite his injuries, pilot Flt Lt W. Reid continued to the target, dropped the bomb load and flew the Lancaster back to make a safe landing. Flt Lt Reid was awarded the Victoria Cross: 'his tenacity and devotion to duty was beyond praise'.

Z
XV574
BT
53TFS
AF790053
NATO TIGERS
HARD TO BE HUMBLE
BOMBER COMMAND
ROYAL AIR FORCE
STRIKE HARD STRIKE SURE
LM360

Trimming Decals

All waterslide decals are covered with a varnish coat which is usually much larger than the actual marking. It will show up on your finished model and is therefore best removed by trimming around the marking with a scalpel, whilst still attached to the complete decal sheet. You don't need to cut right through the backing paper because the varnish is very thin and the surrounding excess part will come away when soaked in water.

Attaching Decals

Decals should be soaked thoroughly in luke warm (never hot!) water.

Attaching Decals

Once the marking is completely loose from its backing sheet it should be slid on to the model surface.

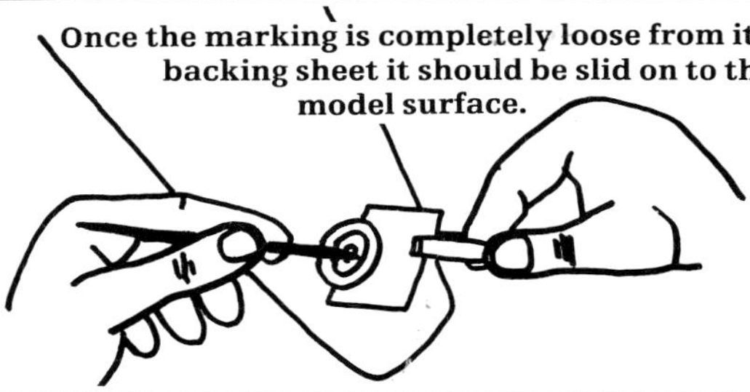

Hasegawa's F11 Tiger, built almost 'straight from the box' with no additional details apart from new markings from a Scalemaster decal sheet.

with a sharp knife to remove any excess carrier varnish that surrounds the marking. If you do not, the decal will dry with a large surround of decal film (varnish) that will stand proud from the model surface and do nothing to add to the realism of the model. If you cut away as much as possible the film will not be so evident. Another problem with leaving decal film around a marking is that the unnecessary varnish is likely to collect small air bubbles beneath it, which will spoil the effect of the decal when dry. The smaller the amount of decal you have to apply to the kit surface, the better the chances are that the dried marking will sit firmly on the model and look realistic, ie like paintwork. Many kits have a large number of tiny 'stencil' markings, which literally cover almost every part of the model. You should avoid applying all these in one go, as you are likely to inadvertently damage or remove markings whilst applying others. It is far wiser to apply a few at a time.

To aid the application of decals, setting solutions (commonly known as 'Micro' solutions, after the brand name of the first manufacturer of these chemicals) can be bought from many model shops or by mail order from larger hobby suppliers. The use of these setting agents is thoroughly described on the bottle, in the form of instructions, but the basic principle is to apply the decal as normal, adding a few drops of the setting and solvent solution to the decal in order to soften the decal varnish and pull the marking tightly down on to the paint, eventually glueing the marking permanently in place. These agents are particularly useful for sticking decals to curved areas where under normal circumstances a decal marking would be reluctant to adhere. Once all the decals have dried, the setting solutions often leave stains around the markings, but these can be washed off with water, the decals being in no danger of damage as they will now be attached firmly to the surface.

Once all the decals are in place and all are dry, you are free to paint on the final surface finish of your choice. You can use a normal varnish (either oil-based or acrylic) and either hand paint or spray. A better finish will be obtained with a spray can or air brush, but this is by no means essential. Apart from restoring the desired sheen (gloss, matt or semi-matt), the final coat will seal all the decals under a protective coat which will avoid causing damage to them at any later stage. Many modellers prefer to use specific model clear finishes that are designed for such uses. They are much less thick than normal model varnish, dry far more rapidly and often provide a far more durable finish. Available in either gloss or matt, it is a simple matter to mix a combination of the two to obtain a semi-matt (or satin) effect. Like the setting solutions, you may find that you have to purchase these by mail order from larger model suppliers. Very occasionally you may come across 'dry decals' which do not need to be soaked in water. These are rubbed-down on to the surface and are instantly secure. You will find that these (albeit rather rare) markings are prone to damage, and the final clear coat of varnish is essential to protect them.

Once all the decals have been applied successfully and sealed in a final coat of varnish, you may well decide that your model is complete. There is at least one more consideration you could give to your model, and that is 'whether to weather'. 'Weathering' is a term used by modellers to describe the dirt and stains that are common to real aircraft. Unless an aircraft has just rolled out from the paint shop it is likely to be covered with dirt, oil streaks, etc, and in places the paint will have faded in colour. Civil aircraft and airliners in particular are often kept in superb condition, and it is really only military aircraft that are allowed to become very dirty, chiefly because they have no passengers to impress. Unfortunately, no kit instruction sheet will tell you where and how to apply such effects, and the only alternative is to look at real aircraft and try to copy what you see. Photographs are essential, be they your own pictures or illustrations in a book or magazine. Look for some pictures of the aircraft type you are modelling, and examine the aircraft surface. Is it really completely clean? It probably is not, so it is vital to check exactly where the dirt and stains appear, as they often vary from aircraft to aircraft. The most obvious place where dirt appears is around the engines, especially around the exhaust area, where either soot from jet engines or oil from piston engines will stain the aircraft surface; another is around the wheels, where oil stains appear, and mud often splashes from the ground. Whilst observing where stains often appear, you should note that all dirt will almost inevitably appear in patches which run in line with the airflow over the aircraft surface.

There are many ways of simulating dirt on a model, and often it is a matter of personal choice as to how one recreates such effects. By far the easiest method is by spraying streaks of thinned grey/black paint through an air brush. If you have to depend on a paint brush, applying thinned black paint with a brush will probably overdo the whole effect, and the best approach is to attempt 'dry-brushing'. This is done by dipping your brush in an appropriate 'oily' colour and then wiping the brush clean on a tissue. Once the brush appears to be dry there will be a minute residue of paint left on the brush, and if you lightly dust the model surface with the brush you will find that a very slight staining effect can be achieved. It is important to keep the brush dry, otherwise you will streak patches of paint along the kit surface. A patient and slow process of gradual application will give the best result.

Another variation on the dry-brushing technique is to use pencil lead on your brush, instead of paint. Sand some pencil lead on to your abrasive paper and rub your brush into the dust. You will find that this dust can be applied to the model in much the same

Above:
Something of an antique, this Airfix Ford Trimotor shows how decals have been applied over the airframe's corrugated surface and have adhered successfully thanks to the use of a decal softening solution. *Ron Firth/Pamag Publications*

Above:
A 1/32nd scale F-4J Phantom built from a rather old and basic Revell kit. The use of a specialist decal sheet has provided some colourful markings and the dozens of small stencilled instructional markings that were once found in very large numbers on such aircraft. Nowadays only the more important markings are retained. The mirror base reveals some subtle weathering on the underside.

Above:
Note the 'tip-toed' appearance of the undercarriage on this Monogram F-20 Tigershark (1/48th scale), caused by using the wheels straight from the box instead of sanding away a portion of the tyre's lower surfaces. *Monogram*

Left:
Monogram's 1/48th scale A-10 Thunderbolt II shows the wing-tip speed brakes to full advantage, in their open positions. This feature is unique to this kit, and the same configuration would present a difficult scratch-building task in any other A-10 kit. *Monogram*

Below:
Monogram's 1/72nd scale B-1B displays the swing-wing feature to full advantage. Most kits of 'swingers' incorporate gears that allow the wings to be moved, although inevitably this leads to a slight loss of authenticity, as the wing-to-fuselage seal cannot be represented properly; nor can the extended wing flaps and slats which normally hang open when the aircraft is on the ground. *Monogram*

way as dry-brushed paint, but with pencil lead you can easily wipe away mistakes with a damp cloth and start again. Of course, the model will have to be given a coat of varnish to seal the pencil stains, so it would be best to consider this method before applying the final coat of varnish.

Another common aspect of weathering is the fading effect air and sun has upon paintwork. Depending on the type of paint and the prevailing conditions, paint will gradually fade to a lighter colour with age, and many aircraft readily illustrate this effect on close inspection. Often the fading varies over the aircraft surface, between different metal panels. The fading can easily be recreated on your model with an air brush by carefully spraying patches of airframe with a 'faded' version of the original aircraft colour (add a few drops of white to the original paint to give the faded effect). For non-air brush modellers a similar finish can be achieved by dry-brushing an area with a faded paint. You may also notice that on some aircraft the lines between the many metal panels have become very evident and often appear as a faint 'patchwork' of lines over the airframe. This too can be imitated on your model. Most kits feature a representation of the airframe panel lines, often with inscribed detail or sometimes with raised lines. If your kit has raised lines you might well have sanded away most of the detail during the construction process, but it is a fairly straightforward job to re-scribe the lines with a ruler and a blade edge or a proper scribing point. Examination of photographs will show where the main panel lines appear. To highlight the lines, and also the lines between the moving control surfaces and the airframe, you can run a line of ink from a draughting pen. As an alternative, use a sharp pencil or try 'washing' an area with a very weak solution of thinned black paint. The paint will run into all the lines and you can then wipe the surface with a cloth dampened in thinners. This will leave behind just the highlighted panel lines. Of course, this process really needs to be practised and only a small area should be attempted at a time. Also, you should have already, given the model a coat of varnish, otherwise the paint wash could stain the main finish.

Yet another effect of time and weather on an aircraft is the peeling of small pieces of paintwork, revealing the metal surface or undercoat beneath. You can easily reproduce this on the model by scratching odd places with the point of a knife blade. This will reveal the white undercoat below, which from a distance will look like the silver of the metal airframe. It is important, however, not to get carried away with this and cover the aircraft in chips. Only wartime aircraft sustained large amounts of such damage, most machines having just odd patches (often the wing leading edges) where the airflow has gradually worn away the paintwork. With all types of weathering the effects have to be subtle, not overdone. As usual a little practice will show just how much is right.

The experienced modeller might look towards the more specialised methods of applying markings. One obvious attraction is the vast range of specialist decal sheets that are widely available. These provide markings for aircraft different to those featured in the kit decal sheet. They often provide more detailed markings too, and they are always of a much higher quality. Although a few model shops do sell specialist sheets (such as Microscale) they are more easily obtained from large mail order suppliers who will supply a list of sheets available on request. Once any modeller has become familiar with the hobby it is natural to want to try something a little different, and the desire to model an aircraft that is unique to the builder is quite common. The only way that one can vary the aircraft one is attempting to model is to change the markings thus representing another aircraft to that depicted in the kit. Specialist decal sheets allow one to do this and are consequently very popular. Even more enthusiastic modellers choose to model

Below:
Matt paint *1* will not accept decals easily. A decal marking will not secure firmly to the matt surface *2* as the microscopic rough surface will allow small air pockets to form under the decal, which will show as a 'silvering' effect, and will not allow the decal to adhere to the surface. A gloss paint surface *3* will have a much better effect, as it is much smoother and thus avoids the air-pocket problem. However, with the aid of a decal softening solution the decal will 'melt' and conform to the surface. Small air bubbles can be burst with a pin, and more setting solution applied *4*. A coat of varnish, even a thin one, will seal the decal and protect it from damage *5*.

Securing Decals

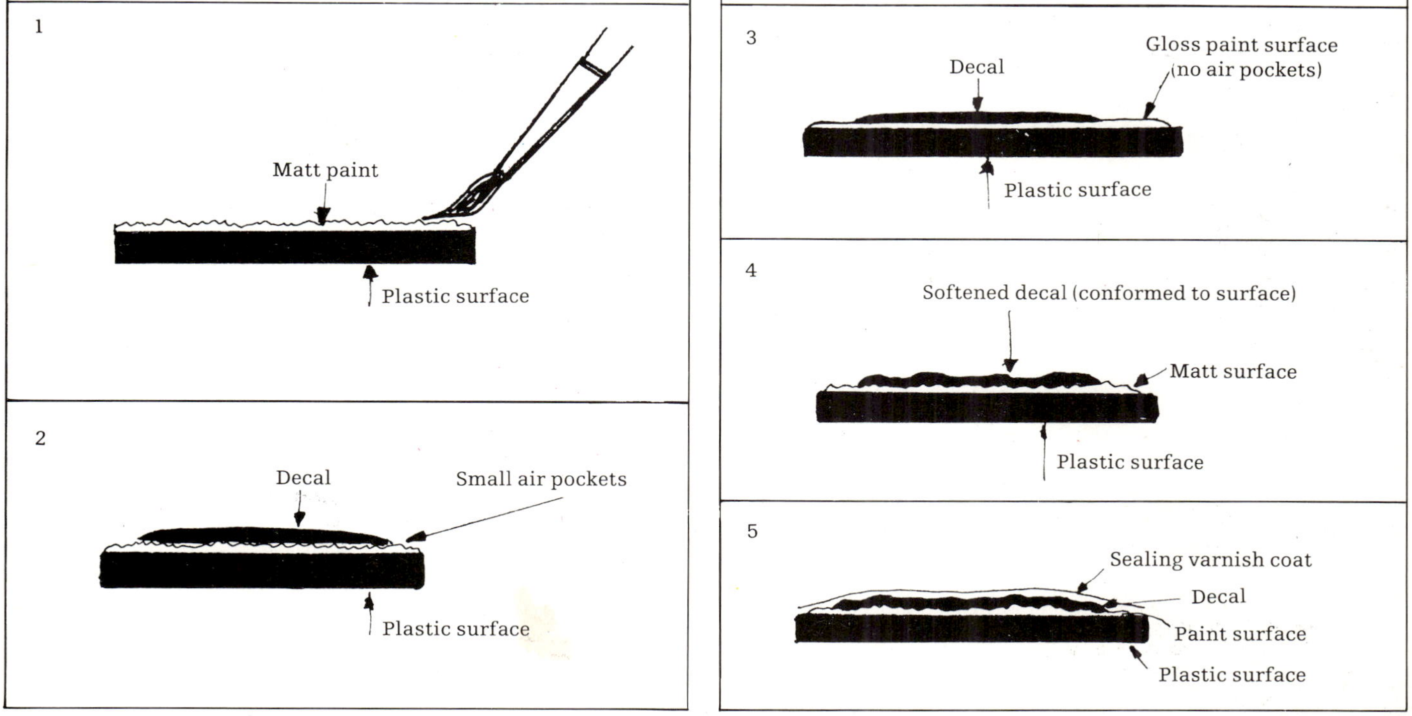

Securing Decals

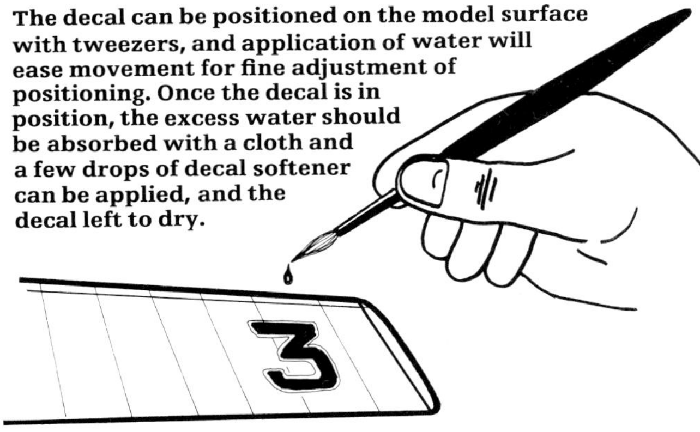

The decal can be positioned on the model surface with tweezers, and application of water will ease movement for fine adjustment of positioning. Once the decal is in position, the excess water should be absorbed with a cloth and a few drops of decal softener can be applied, and the decal left to dry.

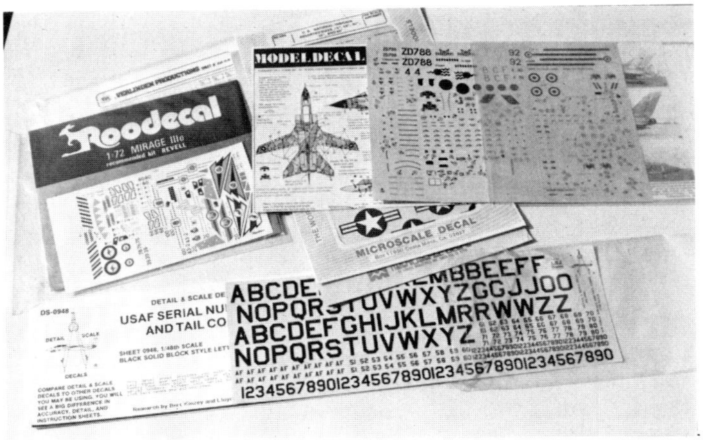

Above right:
Specialist decals are produced by many companies, just a small selection being seen here. There are few colour scheme and marking variations which haven't been covered on at least one decal sheet. Even civilian airliner schemes are well represented, and the desire to represent an aircraft other than that portrayed in the kit can easily be satisfied.

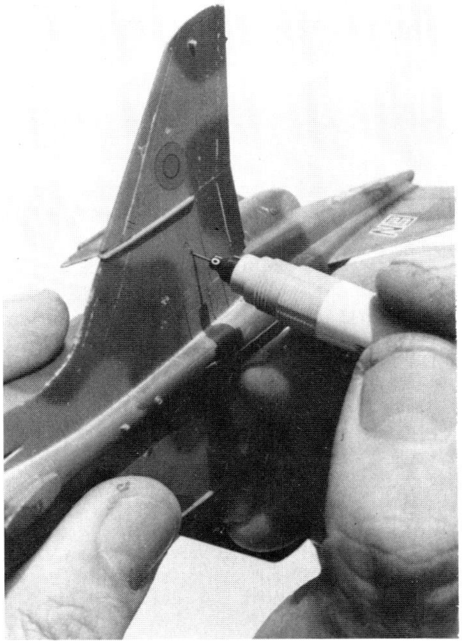

Right:
Engraved panel lines can be highlighted with pencil or, for a more bold effect, with a draughting pen as illustrated. Excess ink can be wiped away with a damp cloth.

Above:
A T-33 built from the Hasegawa kit, with markings from a specialist decal sheet.

Above:
Here two unique shapes in aircraft design are represented by an Italeri 1/72nd scale kit of the B-58 Hustler (foreground) and a Hasegawa kit of the SR-71 in the background. Visible on the SR-71 are panel line weathering highlights which add to the realism of the finished creation.

an aircraft for which a decal sheet simply does not exist. This leaves no option other than painting the tiny markings by hand. There are two approaches that give acceptable results, the most obvious being to paint markings directly on to a model. Whilst this is possible (with lots of practice), a slightly easier method is to paint the markings on to a sheet of 'clear' decal. This type of decal sheet can also be obtained and is simply a sheet of clear varnish on to which you can first draw and then paint your markings, after which they can be applied to the model like a normal decal. Obviously this approach allows you to accurately draw your markings before painting them and applying them to your model. Another useful accessory is the range of solid colour decal sheets, large blocks of one colour which can be cut to whatever shape you need. The most difficult, and yet the most effective way of painting markings, is to copy the full-size machine and spray the markings through paper (or sticky tape) stencils which have to be carefully pre-cut with a very sharp knife. Of course, this is a job for an experienced modeller and should not be attempted by the novice. In any case, such approaches are very rarely needed, as almost any marking one can imagine is available on at least one decal sheet — somewhere!

Reproducing realism

The main requirement of any model (as opposed to a simple toy) is that it should accurately represent the full-size real example, and consequently one of the chief aspects of aircraft modelling is reproducing realism. Apart from a range of modelling skills, there is another important talent needed in order to consistently reproduce realistic models, and this is an eye for detail. It is easy to look at a pile of aircraft photographs or to stare at a full-size aeroplane without really looking at it at all. You must remember to look for details rather than the overall picture. Take for example a Tornado GR1 which you have just built straight from the box without performing any extra tasks other than those mentioned on the kit instruction sheet. You will have a very attractive model no doubt, but is it as good as it could be? Take a look at some photographs of a real Tornado, and look carefully at what you see, and then make some critical comparisons with your model. First of all, you must notice that the real aircraft is not parked on a wooden shelf or hanging from the sky on an enormous piece of string! It is parked on a concrete hardstanding, which is either made from huge square slabs of light brown-coloured material or a smooth dark grey tarmac surface. The floor is not one uniform colour either, as it is soaked with oil stains, scuff marks, tyre marks and so on. If the aircraft you are looking at is on display at an air show the floor is surely covered with trash of all kinds, ranging from fizzy drink cans to sweet wrappers. If, however, you are looking at an operational airfield there certainly will not be any loose items on the floor. Even before actually examining the aircraft, you have your first lesson in realism laid before you.

Now take a look at the aircraft itself, and examine it carefully. The most obvious area that will contain far more detail than your model will be the cockpit, which will be crammed full of dials, instruments, switches, pipes and much more. Of course, every aircraft has a different cockpit layout, so it is essential to have a good look at the particular aircraft type you are modelling. The main instrument panels will probably be represented as small decal markings in your kit, but before you happily use these items look at the real instrument panel. It is not a flat board with black and white circles scattered across it, is it? In fact it is a whole cluster of individual instrument dials and switches, all of different shapes and sizes gathered together on the main panel. The main point to notice is that the instrument panel is never simply a flat surface, so in order to give even just a hint of realism you must change your model panel into a three-dimensional piece. To be fair, some kits now include panels that do represent this area more effectively, with a proper moulded panel that does not rely on a decal for effect. In these kits you will have to pick out all the instruments with your paint brush; to obtain the correct

Below left:
With the addition of new accessories, Tim Perry has created this realistic scene based on an Airfix $^1/_{72}$nd scale Hawk. Note how the flaps have been cut out and extended downwards, the detail added to the cockpit, and the neat canopy framing achieved by using strips of white decal cut to shape. *Tim Perry*

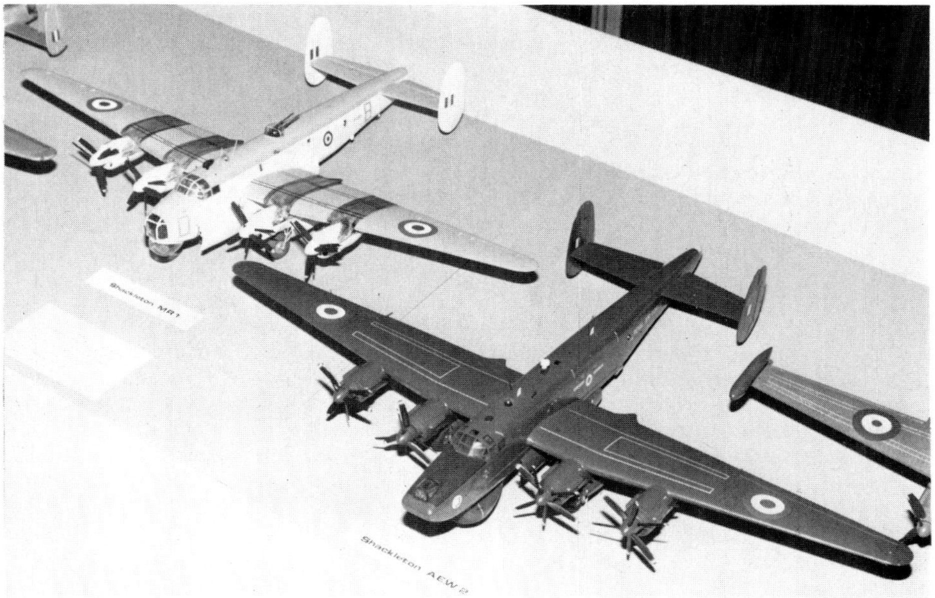

Below:
These Shackletons were both extensively modified from the elderly (and rare) Frog kit. The aircraft in the foreground is an AEW2 which features large single mainwheels and a tailwheel, as compared to the smaller twin mainwheels and nose undercarriage featured in the Frog kit which portrays a MR3. The large nose radome has also been scratch-built. The aircraft in the background is even more extensively modified and represents a MR1 with a narrow glazed nose section, clear radome and fuselage turret.

Above:
A $^1/_{72}$nd scale F-101 Voodoo, made from the Matchbox kit but heavily modified and improved. Much detail has been added, such as the scratch-built radar in the nose, detailed cockpit and extended flaps. The mirror base helps to display the underside and the missiles buried in the weapons bay.

Above right:
A Hawker Typhoon showing some very effective weathering in the form of chipped paintwork and dark exhaust staining.

colours for each tiny item you will again have to refer to a photograph of the real thing. Alternatively, for an effect that is almost as authentic, you can simply paint the whole panel matt black, and when it is dry, 'dry-brush' the surface with matt white paint which will highlight all the delicate moulded detail without you having to paint every individual item. The overall effect is quite good and much easier to achieve, but it does assume that the panel is simply black and white (rarely the case!).

Unfortunately the vast majority of kits still have just decal sheets for the instrument panels, so you are left to build your own panel from scratch. You will probably have a flat surface with which to start adding your details, and the decal might well provide an indication of where the dials and switches should be, but even this is something of an assumption in some kits that simply include fictitious items. Once again, a photograph will reveal all! To make the instruments into three-dimensional objects you need to produce a number of tiny squares of plastic, through which a hole can be drilled, in order to represent the typical instrument dial surround. Thankfully, this is not such a difficult task, as many model stores sell packs of variously-sized thin plastic strips from which small squares can be cut. Miniature drills can be purchased too, and for such delicate items the drill turning power is easily provided by finger and thumb, so this is not such an expensive prospect. These instrument surrounds can then be stuck on to the main panel and painted black. The circular faces can be painted in a contrasting grey, or for those with an eye for extreme detail, small white dial markings can be picked out with a (very) fine paint brush or, better still, a needle used in the same fashion. If the plastic instrument face is made in white plastic, the small white details can be scratched in etching fashion with a needle, through the matt black paint. Another recent development saves a great deal of work, albeit at a price, as ready-made instrument surrounds can now be purchased from model suppliers.

One other obvious feature of instrument panels is the array of tiny switches that appear in every corner. These are best represented by small stems of thin plastic that can be obtained at no cost by cutting sections from a piece of stretched plastic sprue. With the aid of a miniature drill, make holes in the appropriate places on the instrument panel, insert a strand of plastic, cement it in place (from the rear of the panel) and, when dry, cut the stem down to produce a small hair-sized switch that can then be painted.

Looking away from the main instrument panels, down each side of the cockpit walls, you will see yet more switches as well as the power control throttles on the left-hand side. Depending on the age/quality of the kit you are using, you may find that these side consoles are either completely absent from the kit (in which case they will have to be constructed from plastic card and detailed as the main instrument panels) or shown as flat boxes on to which more instrument and switch decals are meant to be added. Again, if you want to give the full effect of realism you are best advised to ignore decals and aim for a three-dimensional look. If you are lucky to have a recent kit you may well find that all details are provided.

The pilot's seat is another item that is commonly ignored by kit manufacturers and is rarely anything like a real seat. In the case of our example (the Tornado) the two seats are Martin Baker Mk 10 ejection seats which by their very nature are complicated pieces of engineering and not a couple of armchairs as many kit items would have you believe. They contain rocket packs, parachutes, oxygen bottles and survival equipment, all of which (and more) can be seen when examining a cockpit photograph. Unless you are particularly skilled you will not be inclined to build your own seats from scraps of plastic; and luckily you do not have to, as manufacturers such as Aeroclub produce fully detailed seats from cast white metal. One or two details will still need to be added, mostly in the form of piping (made from fuse wire or stretched plastic sprue), and the most important item is always overlooked: this is the ejection seat firing handle, which is normally located at the base of the seat between the pilot's legs, although older types of seat also have handles on the top of the seats. They are inevitably painted with black/yellow stripes and are essential additions to any seat, modelled from wire or stretched plastic.

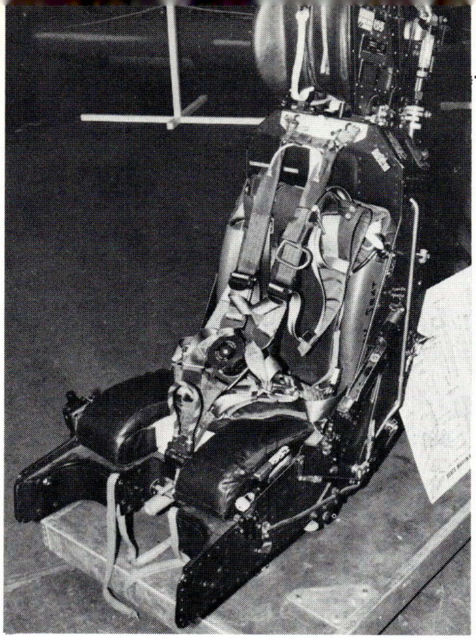

Above:
Ejection seats are much more detailed than many kit seats would suggest. This Jaguar seat illustrates the fact clearly, and to add to a model's accuracy such details have to be considered. Rather than building new seats from scratch, most seats can be purchased from specialist suppliers such as Aeroclub, which produces white metal seats in $^1/_{48}$th and $^1/_{72}$nd scales for many aircraft, all of which incorporate the majority of seat details.

On top of the basic seat structure there is the parachute and harness equipment which must be added. In the case of parachute packs (when fitted), they can be shapes formed from pieces of plastic or epoxy modelling putty. Seat straps can be cut from sticky tape, first painted the appropriate colour. The strap ends will carry a buckle of some sort which can be represented by suitably shaped fuse wire, although even these tiny items can be purchased ready-made in detail packs. The colour of the various seat details will vary from seat to seat, so you will again have to rely on a photograph. Looking upwards slightly, you will notice that the canopy will carry rear view mirrors (just like your car!) and these should be made from plastic scrap or taken from an appropriate detailing set such as that provided by the best known manufacturer, PP Aeroparts.

These then, are the basic details common to the cockpits of many modern jets; minor variations are many, and older piston-engine types are different again, but thankfully rather less complicated! One other point to remember is that pilots will often leave their helmets, oxygen masks, life jackets, maps and flight information books in their cockpits, and the addition of such items to your model will give it that elusive 'lived-in' appearance. Taking a look outside the cockpit, there will be an access ladder of some sort, either a purpose-built type for the aircraft (the Tornado has its own specific ladder) or a standard RAF stepladder. Some aircraft have built-in steps which extend from the fuselage side when required. Although it is possible to build such items from scratch, PP Aeroparts has a very extensive range of ladders for many aircraft which can be purchased from model shops. They are made from etched brass sheet and are cut out, bent to shape and stuck together with 'superglue'. Because the access ladder is moved regularly, stood upon and so on, these items are always very dirty, with chipped paintwork and scuff marks. Quite often the aircraft fuselage is in a similar state at the point where the ladder meets the aircraft and where the pilots and ground crew regularly stand (the ledge surrounding the cockpit wall is a favourite place for such damage).

Looking at the external surface of the aircraft, you will see that it is not simply a case of two coats of camouflage colours. The Tornado, for instance, features an overall camouflage of grey and green, but have a look in detail at the exact shades of grey and green. It is no good taking two tins of model paint and expecting to create an exact replica of the real paint scheme, it just is not that easy. The two basic colours will have been fairly uniform in shade when first applied in the factory paint shop, but since then the constant exposure to rain, airflow and sunshine, will have caused the paint to fade in areas such as the leading edges of the wings and fins. Some access panels will have been removed and replaced by panels from other aircraft which may have a slightly different shade of colour. Sometimes, because the camouflage scheme pattern is not followed too closely by the painters, some aircraft will be green in one area whilst an identical aircraft will be painted grey in the same spot. Thus the common practice of changing access panels regularly results in a patchwork of different paint colours. The Tornado F2 fighter, painted in an Air Defence grey colour scheme, has often been seen with tailplane leading edges that have been taken from GR1s, painted in dark grey/green. To make matters even more complicated, repairs to the airframe surface are often overpainted with a spray of the appropriate colour. Because tins of paint rarely contain identical colours, the patches of new paint can sometimes be slightly different in hue, especially if applied on to an aircraft that carries time-faded paint! Added to all this is the continual chipping of paintwork around access panels where screwdrivers have gone astray, or where groundcrew boots have damaged the surface. Quite often 'visitors' will have 'zapped' the aircraft with stickers of various descriptions, applied in all sorts of places. The more

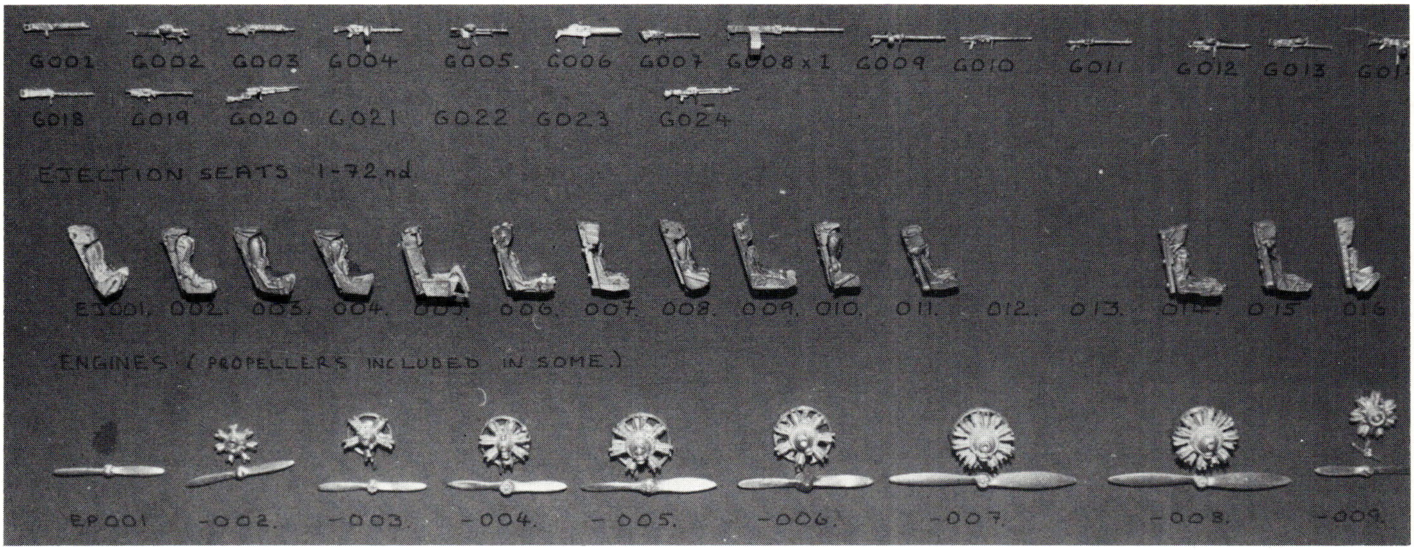

Part of the Aeroclub cast white metal range, showing some of the $^1/_{72}$nd scale ejection seats, machine guns, engines and propellers which are available.

Above:
A 1/48th scale Sea Harrier based on the Airfix kit, but with added improvements such as the access ladder.

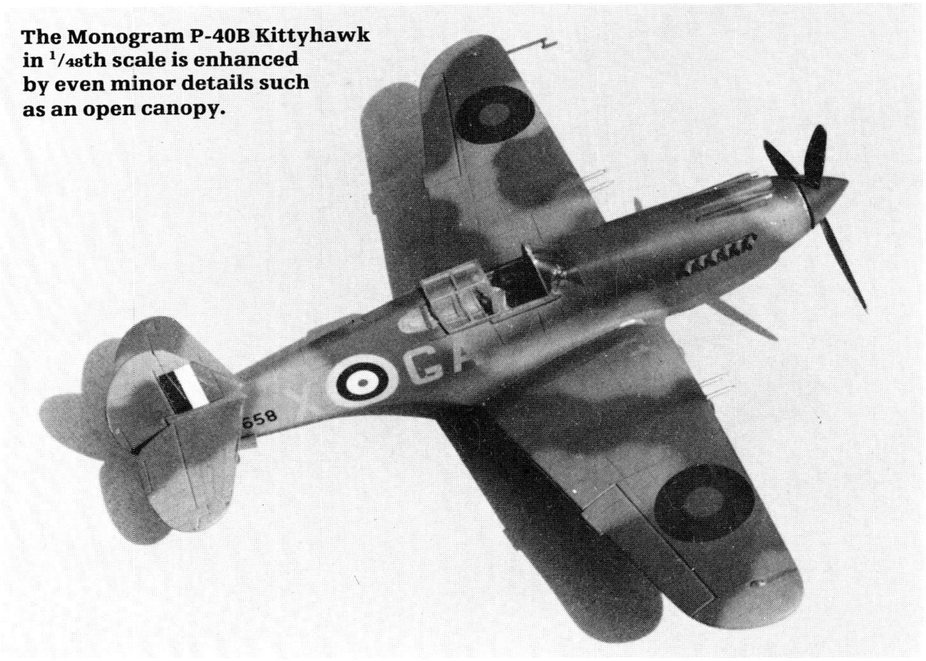

The Monogram P-40B Kittyhawk in 1/48th scale is enhanced by even minor details such as an open canopy.

adventurous have been known to paint slogans or cartoons, etc, on aircraft, and few military aircraft escape this sort of activity. Even when such damage is cured, the tell-tale signs of repair show up, due to the variations in paint hue. A famous example is that of a Tornado that had clearly sported the French word 'Merde' in large letters across the fuselage side. Even careful repainting of the aircraft in the damaged parts still could not hide the offending word!

Cosmetic appearances aside, the physical state of the aircraft can also be examined. Looking at our example Tornado, you might well notice the obvious position of the variable-position wings, but there's much more to observe. In almost every instance the wings are fully forward when at rest, and apart from very rare events, the trailing-edge wing flaps and leading edge slats will be extended downwards. No kit offers you this option, so you will have to resort to some careful cutting and plastic card-building in order to portray the very complicated flaps and slats, together with their clearly visible actuating jacks. Most modern aircraft will be seen with flaps and slats extended (not least airliners), and representing such control surfaces is almost always a do-it-yourself task, as very few kits offer such facilities. The tailplanes may be turned upwards or downwards, the rudder may be turned to the left or right — all important little points. In the case of the Tornado, one of the most characteristic features of this aircraft is the large amount of soot staining across the lower fin, caused by the jet engine exhaust being blown back across this area when the thrust reversers are used on landing. Aircraft often have their own peculiar places where dirt or oil staining tends to gather. The Buccaneer often has an almost black area around the rear fuselage, close to the jet pipe exhausts. The Vulcan was famous for the filthy stains around the lower surfaces of the engine fairings, and even the modern F-18 Hornet carries large deposits of soot staining around the nose gun ports.

Moving to the undersurfaces, the undercarriage often suffers from excessive oil and mud staining, depending on the aircraft type. One thing that will be clear on inspection of any landing gear is that kits rarely if ever correctly portray the vast amount of minor detail that is found in this area. The landing gear carries brake pipes, shock absorbing legs and pipes, landing lights, jack points and much more. Adding extra detail is again a time-consuming job that has to be done with the aid of photographs. The tyres are another point of interest. They often carry tread marks, which are generally ignored in the kit examples. The tyres are not circular either, as the inspection of even a simple car tyre will show how the lower portions will bulge outwards under any weight. Certainly it is wise to remove a small portion of the tyre surface to give a flat base, but the more adventurous would be wise to consider adding slight bulges to each side of the tyre base, made from small touches of filler. However, a note of caution: some aircraft types have high pressure tyres that don't show any sign of bulging, and hardly show a flat surface against the ground, the F-104 Starfighter being an example. Colour too is worthy of note, as most will simply paint tyres matt black, but are tyres really this colour? More often they are dark grey, and whilst a matt finish seems sensible, there are circumstances in which gloss black would be a good choice. This is when aircraft have been specially prepared for exhibition and the paint shop has actually painted the tyres gloss black! It does happen, so check first! Looking into the undercarriage bays will reveal another area that is neglected by kit manufacturers. Almost any gear well includes a vast array of piping, together with various tanks and boxes, usually covered with oil or mud. The undercarriage doors are worthy of consideration too; they do not simply 'stick' to the fuselage on the real aircraft, they are attached by hinges and actuating jacks. In some cases you could save much detailing work by leaving the undercarriage doors in the raised position, as many types have doors which only open for gear movement, and then close again. However, this old 'dodge' is not strictly legitimate, as after a short amount of time on the ground, most gear doors open due to the gradual bleeding-off of pneumatic pressure.

If you build a model that carries weaponry of any kind you'll find that whilst on the ground the bombs, missiles, etc, carry safety pins that effectively disarm the weapons until take-off. These safety pins are connected to large ribbons known as 'remove before flight' tags because they often carry these words on them for the benefit of ground crew, who pull out the pins just before take-off. The tags are either red or bright orange, or even red/white striped, and can be found in various positions on weaponry of all kinds. Missiles often have plastic or wooden caps that fit over their nose sections whilst on the ground, and again they will carry tags. Even the basic airframe will sport a selection of tags, especially on undercarriage legs, and on pitot tubes which always have cloth covers whilst on the ground. Their precise position, of course, varies between aircraft types. These tags are easily made from sticky tape or, better still, from coloured decal sheet cut to shape. Some kits even include such items! One other item that has yet to be included in kits (with the exception of the Hasegawa 1/32nd scale F-16 kit) is the line of static discharge wicks that are attached to the trailing edges of wings, fins and tailplanes on almost every aircraft. They are nothing more than strands of wire that allow static electricity to be easily brushed off the airframe. They are a common feature to most aircraft and can be represented simply by thin plastic strands or even hair. It might appear to be bordering on the trivial, but small details such as these are things that make a model look real. What is very clear, is that no aircraft is as simple to construct as a kit sheet would suggest. Clearly, you would be advised to have some photographs of your subject before you build it, and there's no excuse for not having pictures to hand, as the range of books and magazines available makes a photograph of just about anything you need quite possible, if you just look in the right place!

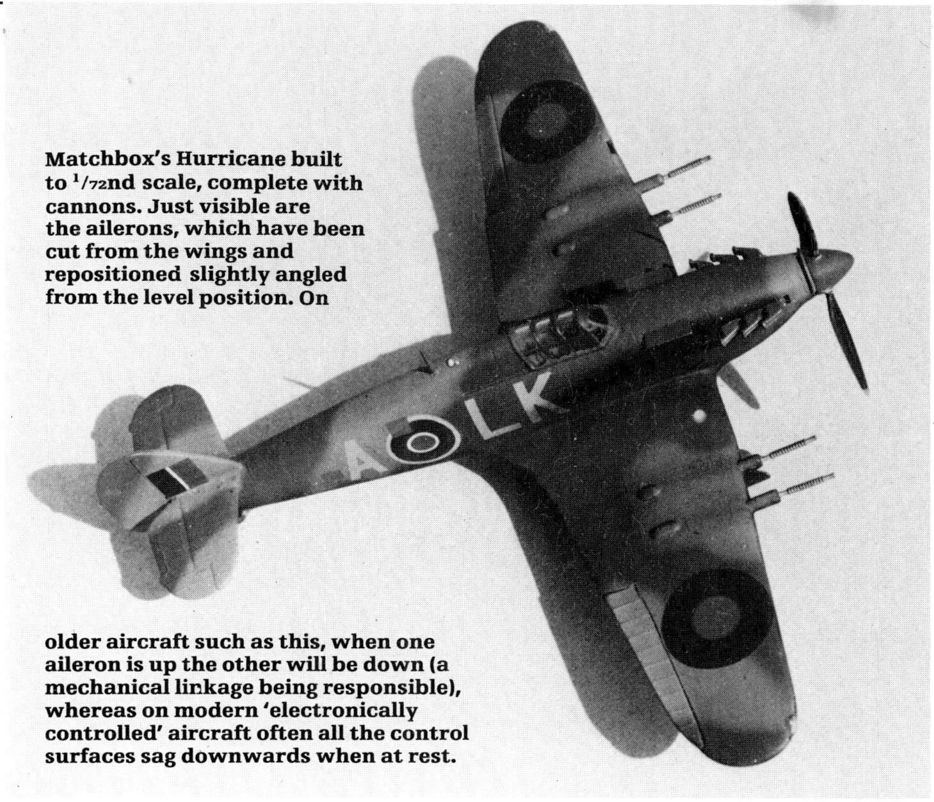

Matchbox's Hurricane built to 1/72nd scale, complete with cannons. Just visible are the ailerons, which have been cut from the wings and repositioned slightly angled from the level position. On older aircraft such as this, when one aileron is up the other will be down (a mechanical linkage being responsible), whereas on modern 'electronically controlled' aircraft often all the control surfaces sag downwards when at rest.

Centre right:
A Fujimi 1/48th scale F-14 Tomcat, devoid of any weathering effect normally found on most US Navy aircraft but equally as valid as a representation of a 'factory fresh' machine.

Bottom right:
Based on a fibreglass travel agent's model, a little detailing and paintwork has produced this 1/72nd scale KC-10.

Details and extras

Over the past few years there has been a great expansion in the range of kit accessories available to the modeller, and for the more enthusiastic model builder the actual plastic kit is only one part of a whole collection of bits and pieces that go together to create a scale replica of an aircraft. The variety of 'extras' that can be purchased to either improve or alter a basic kit is quite staggering, and it would be possible to fill a complete book just describing these items; however, there are some items that even a novice modeller ought to be aware of, right from the beginning of his new hobby. Paints, decal sheets and surface filling putties have been mentioned elsewhere, but there is yet more that can be found to make an average model something special.

Conversion parts are very much part of today's modelling scene. A typical conversion kit consists of a piece of plastic resin which has been moulded to represent a major aircraft component, such as a nose section, that can be used to substitute the same part as supplied in your kit, and thus represent an aircraft of a different mark. For example, conversion parts are available to alter a Panavia Tornado GR1 into a F2 fighter by substituting the blunt nose of the GR1 (as supplied in the kit) for the long, sleek fighter nose. In addition to the larger resin parts, normally supplied are a selection of smaller cast white metal pieces which represent underwing stores (bombs, missiles, ECM pods, etc) together with smaller detailed parts which might not be included in the basic kit, such as tiny aerials, air vent tubes and so on. Taking the Airfix kit of the Canberra as an example, conversion sets are available to provide all the alternative parts for a tandem-seat B-57 and Canberra T17s, TT18s and T22s to name but a few.

On a similar theme, a conversion set to alter the Italeri B-57 kit to a standard RAF Canberra B2 is also available. This latter kit does not feature any metal or resin parts, rather a set of vacuum-formed plastic pieces. Normal plastic kit parts are formed by the injection moulding process which involves pouring plastic (under high pressure) into metal moulds. The vacuum process (known as a 'vacform') takes a piece of sheet plastic which is heated and pulled down over a raised mould whilst still heated. The vacform process does not produce a set of separate three-dimensional components, but a sheet of raised lumps and bumps which have to be cut away from the flat sheet and sanded to their precise shape. Small parts such as undercarriage assemblies cannot be made by the vacform process, but components such as fuselage halves and wings are particularly easy to produce. Because the vacform process if fairly simple and quite inexpensive, many small conversion kits include vacform parts. The method of constructing vacformed items does take a little practice to produce a successful result, and great care is needed in first removing the vacformed shapes from their sheets and then sanding the parts to the final correct shape. However, with practice the use of vacformed

Vacform Kits

Above:
A KC-97 built from a 1/72nd scale Rareplanes kit. The parts for this model are mostly of vacformed sheets, but careful cutting-out and assembly have produced a model which is equally as good as an injection-moulded kit.

Left:
Vacforms represent more of a challenge than normal injection-moulded kits. All parts must be cut carefully from their respective sheets with a sharp knife. It isn't essential to cut completely through each individual piece, as a fairly deep score around their edges will be sufficient to allow one to 'snap' parts from their sheets by careful bending and twisting.

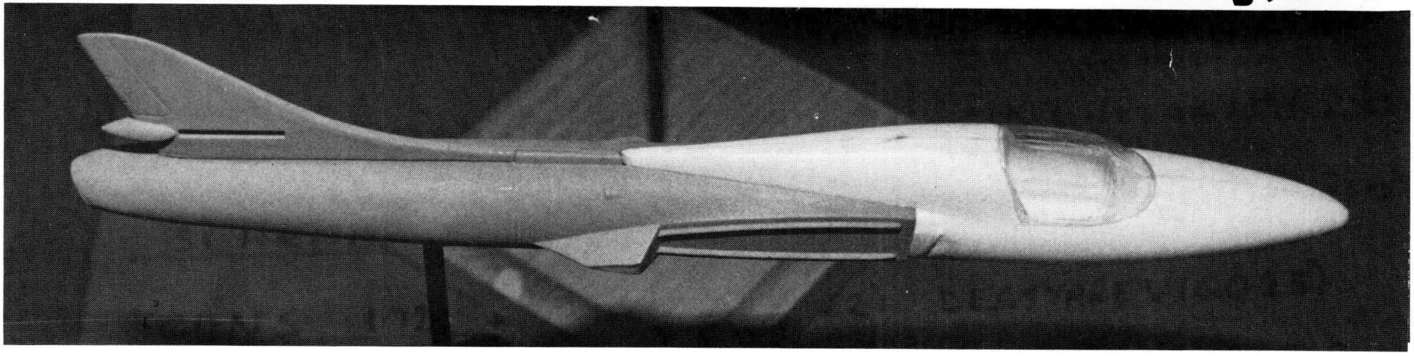

Above:
The Matchbox Hunter (1/72nd scale) includes a twin-seat set of alternative parts, but they are not strictly accurate. Aeroclub Models produces a set of pieces on a vacformed plastic sheet, which when cut out and cemented together make a new forward section for attachment to the Matchbox kit. Alternatively the parts could be mated to an Airfix kit. The canopy is provided on an acetate sheet.

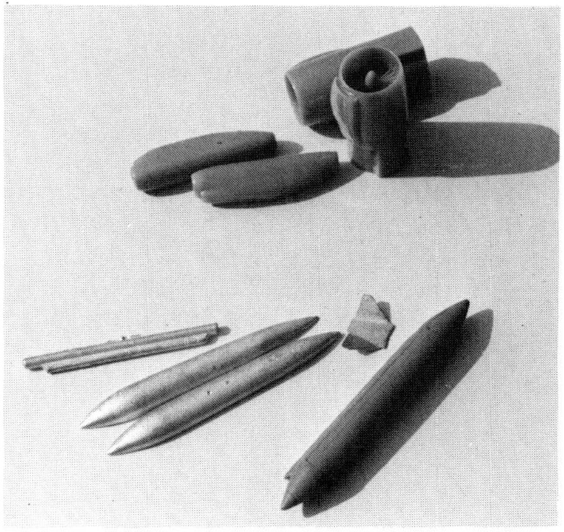

Above:
Metal and resin accessories offer a whole range of variations on specific aircraft subjects. In this picture there are parts from 'C Scale' (foreground) to add underwing tanks, ECM pods or a reconnaissance pod to a Jaguar, all in cast white metal. In the background are Newark Models' resin parts to build a 'big-wing' RB-57 Canberra.

Above:
The B-57B (right) with a later 'big-wing' version shows just two variations on the Canberra theme. Both models started life as Frog/Novo Canberra B(I)8 kits.

parts can become second nature and be no more difficult than working with injection moulded pieces.

Some other conversion sets are produced in a similar fashion, but include only transparent parts to change the glazed portions of a particular aircraft, the cockpit canopy being the usual item. Unlike normal vacformed plastic, the clear transparencies are moulded (in the same way as vacforms) from acetate, which is a very different material to the typical polystyrene that all kits are made from. Acetate cannot be glued with polystyrene cement, as this type of adhesive has absolutely no effect on acetate. Superglue is the most useful type, although you could also use a standard household adhesive (such as 'UHU') which is not quite as permanent as superglue. The process of moulding clear acetate parts is not simply the concern of manufacturers, as more and more modellers have learned the art of canopy moulding. The reason for this particular trend is found in older kits, where the quality or shape of a cockpit canopy is really too bad to be effectively used at all. Sometimes the canopy will not properly fit the fuselage, or (more commonly) it is so thick that it loses all suggestion of realism and is only worth throwing away. As a result many modellers decide to make their own clear parts which will be as accurate as they wish to make them and be much thinner than a moulded plastic part could ever be. Consequently the acetate version will always look more realistic.

The first task in making a canopy is to construct a 'male' mould to the shape of the canopy you require. You can use the original (rejected) piece from the kit as a basis, or start from scratch and carve the shape from a suitably-sized piece of limewood (which can be purchased from any timber suppliers for only a small cost, as the amount required is obviously minimal). The task of carving the shape of a canopy can be time-consuming and tiresome, but the amount of time and care taken in this carving and fine sanding process will be reflected in the final accuracy of the canopy. Once you have the shape that you are looking for, a rough 'female' mould needs to be made. This is a piece of wood into which is cut a hole that is slightly larger than the carved male mould, allowing you to push the male mould cleanly through, with a little room to spare on all sides. The male mould (which you have carved and sanded to the final shape) should be firmly attached to a piece of wooden dowel. This will give you a handle with which to push the piece through the female mould. The next step is to cut a piece of acetate (which should be the thickest that you can find) and attach it to the female mould, with either a staple gun or with drawing pins. The acetate should be centred over the hole with at least a couple of inches of acetate surrounding the hole on all sides. It must be fixed very firmly to the female mould on all sides. Once this is completed you are ready to make your new canopy. The acetate (attached to the female mould) must be heated carefully over a gas stove or electric heater until the acetate becomes floppy. Be sure not to heat it too quickly or it will burn, and don't heat it for too long

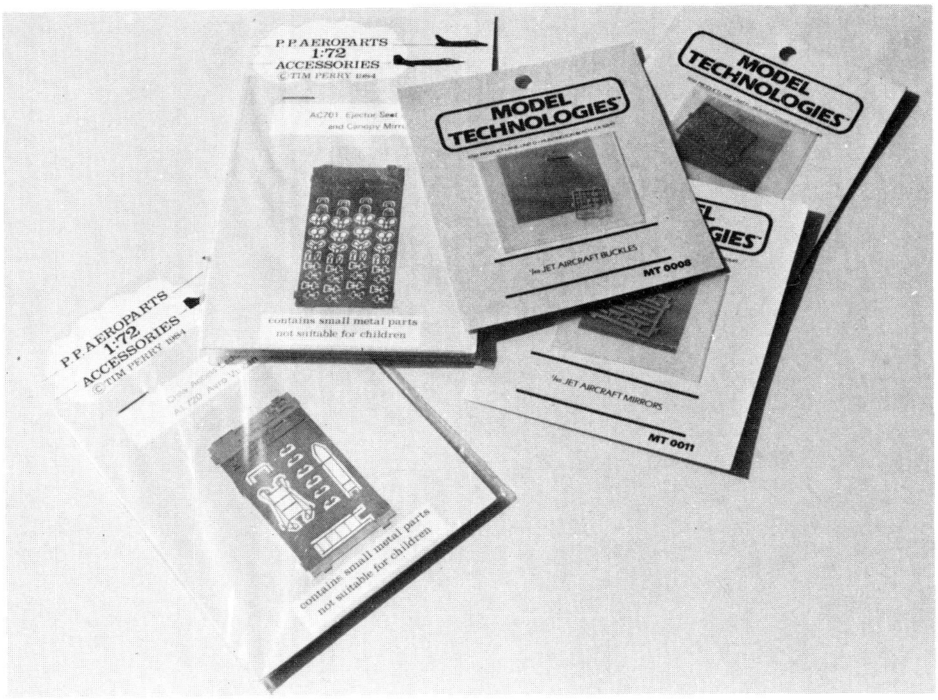

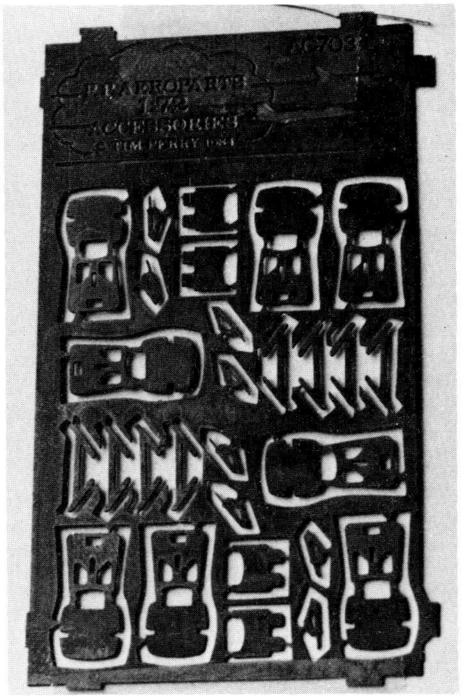

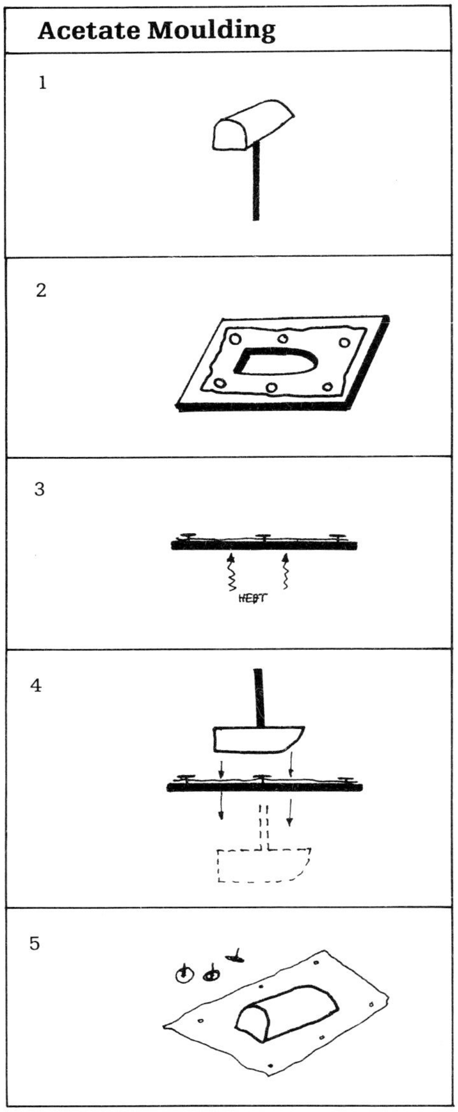

Above:
Photo-etched brass and aluminium parts are fast becoming common and offer many detail parts for addition to aircraft kits. In this picture parts can be seen for a Vulcan access ladder, canopy mirrors and ejection seat handles, seat belt buckles and even instrument surrounds for cockpit panels.

Above right:
Even details such as wheel chocks cannot be overlooked if you are searching for a fully realistic effect. PP Aeroparts produces these etched brass chocks in 1/72nd scale.

Below:
Esci's A-4, with a Roger Saunders cast metal figure, a PP Aeroparts access ladder, all placed on a Verlinden tarmac/concrete base section.

Left:
To mould your own clear canopy, a mould of the desired shape should be made from plastic, Perspex or wood, and firmly attached to a stick for easy handling *1*. A piece of acetate should be pinned firmly to the female mould, covering the canopy-shaped orifice with plenty of surrounding acetate to spare *2*. The acetate should be heated until it is almost ready to bubble *3*, and then the male mould should be quickly pushed through the female mould *4*. After a few moments the acetate will be cool and the canopy (if successful) can be cut away from its surround *5*.

With the aid of various accessories available to the modeller, Tim Perry created this realistic scene based on an Airfix $^1/_{72}$nd scale Tornado kit.

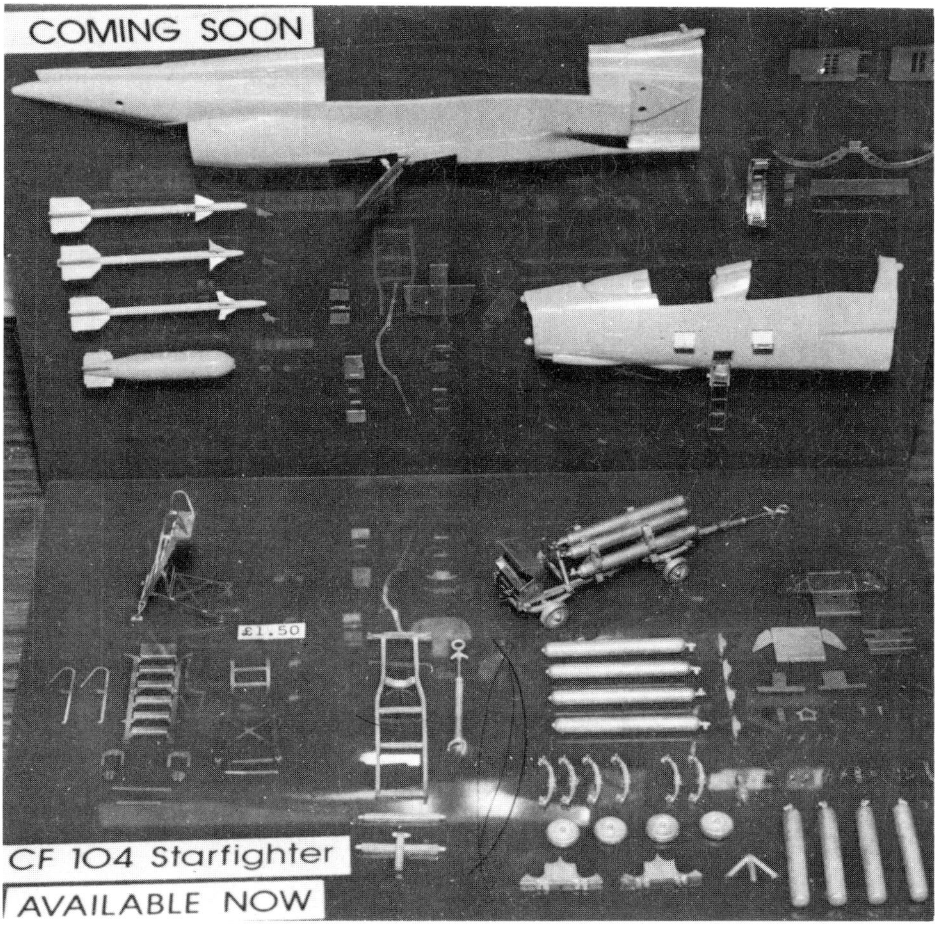

Above:
The range of accessories for aircraft models grows daily. Here is a small part of the PP Aeroparts range which shows such delights as new (and accurate) airbrakes for the Airfix or Hasegawa Jaguar, an access ladder for the Tomcat, missile fins and an oxygen trolley, all to $^1/_{72}$nd scale.

or it will begin to bubble and turn brown. Conversely, don't underheat it or you will not achieve a proper casting. Practice (trial and error!) will show the exact heating time, and fortunately you can afford a few mistakes because acetate sheet isn't too expensive. As soon as the female mould is fully heated, push the male mould quickly through the female mould (starting from the side on which the acetate is pinned) until the mould can go no further, then carefully withdraw it. You will be left with a long, stretched lump of acetate, at the tip of which you will hopefully have a perfect copy of the carved mould. In a few seconds the acetate will be cold and you can cut the new canopy from the surrounding acetate, trimming it carefully to shape after removal. It is fairly certain that your first attempts will not be good enough to use, but just one standard sheet of acetate will allow you to perform perhaps six or so attempts, which will hopefully produce at least one acceptable result. Like every other modelling process, you have to practice. Once this moulding method has been perfected you can use the same process to produce small plastic parts, by substituting thin plastic sheeting for the acetate. With practice you can use the method for making underwing fuel tanks, radomes, etc. Although this is a useful facility, it isn't something that a novice modeller will be eager to try, and providing you stick to building the new high-quality kits you will not have any need even to consider it. It is only when one gets the urge to build older kits that one might find that such steps are desirable.

A very recent development in the

Above:
Rareplanes' vacform Meteor F8, in Israeli markings, on a 'concrete' base. *M. Purchase*

model industry is the advent of etched brass detail parts used for adding extra tiny details to kits. The most famous of these are the PP Aeroparts range of access ladders used on military aircraft. Almost every modern fighter needs a ladder to allow the pilot to reach the cockpit. One or two kits have been known to include ladders with the aircraft, but they are on the whole very rare and usually rather inaccurate. This new range of ladders has become very popular because almost every aircraft that uses a ladder is represented by a particular kit, and all one has to do is to cut out the parts from a brass sheet, bend them to shape along their moulded fold lines and stick them together. With a few coats of paint the flat pieces of brass take on the shape of the rounded metal tubing used on the original. The result is a very authentic ladder that will enhance your model.

The trend towards aircraft accessories does not stop here however, as more and more kits are appearing which include fire extinguishers, wheel chocks, towing tractors, engine starters and even small groundcrew figures. Whilst none of these are actually used to improve the aircraft model, they do look very effective if built into a base display (or 'diorama') on to which you can place your aircraft when completed. Any model will look much more attractive if it is placed on a base of some sort when completed (a piece of polished wood is one favourite), but for a fully authentic effect a small display base will be even more interesting, with ladders, crew, wheel chocks, and so on. Even a suitable runway surface can be purchased, which comes as a sheet of full colour printed card representing the paved concrete of an aircraft dispersal. All you have to do is place the model on top! A less expensive method is to make your own runway from a piece of coloured card (a beige or creamy-brown is about the right concrete colour). You will have to either draw or paint on the paving squares. Another alternative is to paint a piece of plastic sheeting, and at least one manufacturer produces paint in 'concrete' colour specifically for this task. There are yet more etched metal kits available, for canopy mirrors, instrument surrounds (for the cockpit), canopy interior framing, seat belt buckles, and so on: the list is endless. No detail parts are strictly necessary, but for that extra touch of realism, there's nothing to beat them.

Other common accessories are cast metal ones for undercarriage parts (especially vacform kits that otherwise would have none) and ejection seats, which are rarely accurately produced in kits. Apart from the ejection seats, almost all the accessories are produced to $^1/_{72}$nd scale as a reflection of this scale's popularity. Of course, these are further items that have to be considered when you are choosing a scale. Larger $^1/_{48}$th scale kits are supported by limited amounts of conversion and detail kits, but $^1/_{32}$nd and $^1/_{24}$th are not. $^1/_{144}$th scale is also unsupported, not least because the vast majority of kits in this scale are airliners, for which there is little scope for improvement.

One recent development that is of direct benefit to airliner modellers is the arrival of 'Metalcote', a new range of metallic finish paints which can be polished into a full metallic effect. Previously available were some rather expensive pastes which could be applied like polish and had a similar effect, but these latest paints can be painted on like normal enamels (either by brush or spray) and when dry will polish into a very authentic shiny silver finish (bronze, gold and many other variations also being available). Because airliners often feature large areas of natural metal, the new metallic paints are very useful here.

Left:
The vacformed 1/72nd scale kit of the EC-135 produced by Nova Models. This is a big aeroplane to build from a vacform, but what a result!

Below left:
The large but fairly uncomplicated Airfix 1/24th scale Harrier has been altered here to portray the Sea Harrier. The basic alterations are centred around the front, where a revised nose section has been made from plastic card and sanded to shape: the use of internal template structures and strips of plastic 'planking' creates the overall form which is then smoothed to shape with the aid of filler and abrasive paper. The revised canopy has been moulded from acetate sheet. The paint finish is fairly crude, but intentionally so in order to represent the hastily-applied Falklands camouflage used in 1982.

Below:
An airliner in military markings: this is a Bristol Britannia in 1/72nd scale, built from an Airways vacform kit. Considerable detail work has been added to the basic vacformed parts, as well as a scratch-made colour scheme which represents the aircraft formerly operated by A&AEE Boscombe Down.

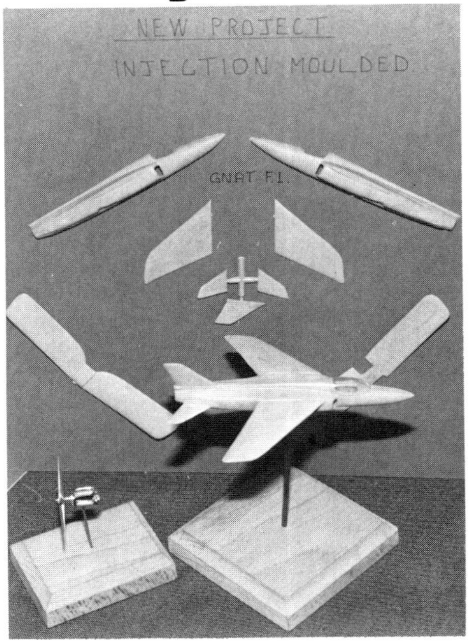

Above:
Aeroclub Models has an ever-expanding range of short-run injection moulded kits which are not as detailed as their more commercial counterparts but easier to build than vacforms. This is a Gnat F1, an aircraft that would never be produced on a full-scale commercial basis because of its limited appeal. The short-run process is the answer.

Above right:
A 1/32nd scale Scorpion built with great skill from a vacform kit.
Ron Firth/Pamag Publications

There is one other 'extra' that is often associated with airliner kits but which has obvious applications for other aircraft too. 'Krystal Kleer' is the brand name of a bottled white liquid solution which can be applied (by cocktail stick) into window orifices and which will dry to a clear, plastic-like finish. On many airliners it can be something of a chore to insert all the clear window parts and having to mask them individually before painting. With this clear drying solution the windows can be left as holes until all the painting is complete. The solution is then applied, and when dry provides a set of clear windows. Granted, the effect is not as authentic as a row of flush-fitting plastic windows, but in the interest of convenience you might well consider this liquid. It also has many other applications, not least for the representation of clear navigation lights on the wing tips and fuselage. For the red or green clear lights, the addition of a drop of food colouring agent will give the solution a suitable tint which will dry clear. As an alternative to the commercial brand solution you could use normal PVA 'white glue' which will work in much the same way.

Conversion and detail sets aside, there are many other items that you might consider for your hobby. Glass, Perspex and plastic display cases are fast becoming very popular. Most are sold as self-assembly kits which fix together in a range of different sizes. They make a useful shield for the finished model, to keep away fingers, vacuum cleaners and dust, all of which are common enemies to a completed model. Electric 'drill' sets are also very common; although inevitably they are expensive, they are ideal for making delicate holes or sawing parts, sanding large difficult pieces of plastic, buffing a paint finish, and so on. Although they can do nothing you can't already do 'by hand', they do make life much easier and are worthy of consideration as birthday/Christmas gifts. A modelling vice is a fairly inexpensive purchase, and while it isn't essential, it can be very useful for holding parts securely and providing an extra 'pair of hands'.

Apart from all these possible purchases, there is one final point which you must remember at all times: never throw any surplus kit parts away! Even the plastic runner sprues should be saved, as the long pieces of plastic are bound to come in useful at some time. More importantly, a piece of runner plastic can be heated and stretched to produce long strands of plastic, which can be used to represent piping, aerial wires or biplane rigging, depending on the thickness to which it is stretched. Just about every kit will leave you with

Above:
The Airfix Vulcan B2, with both Skybolt missiles built from plastic scrap.

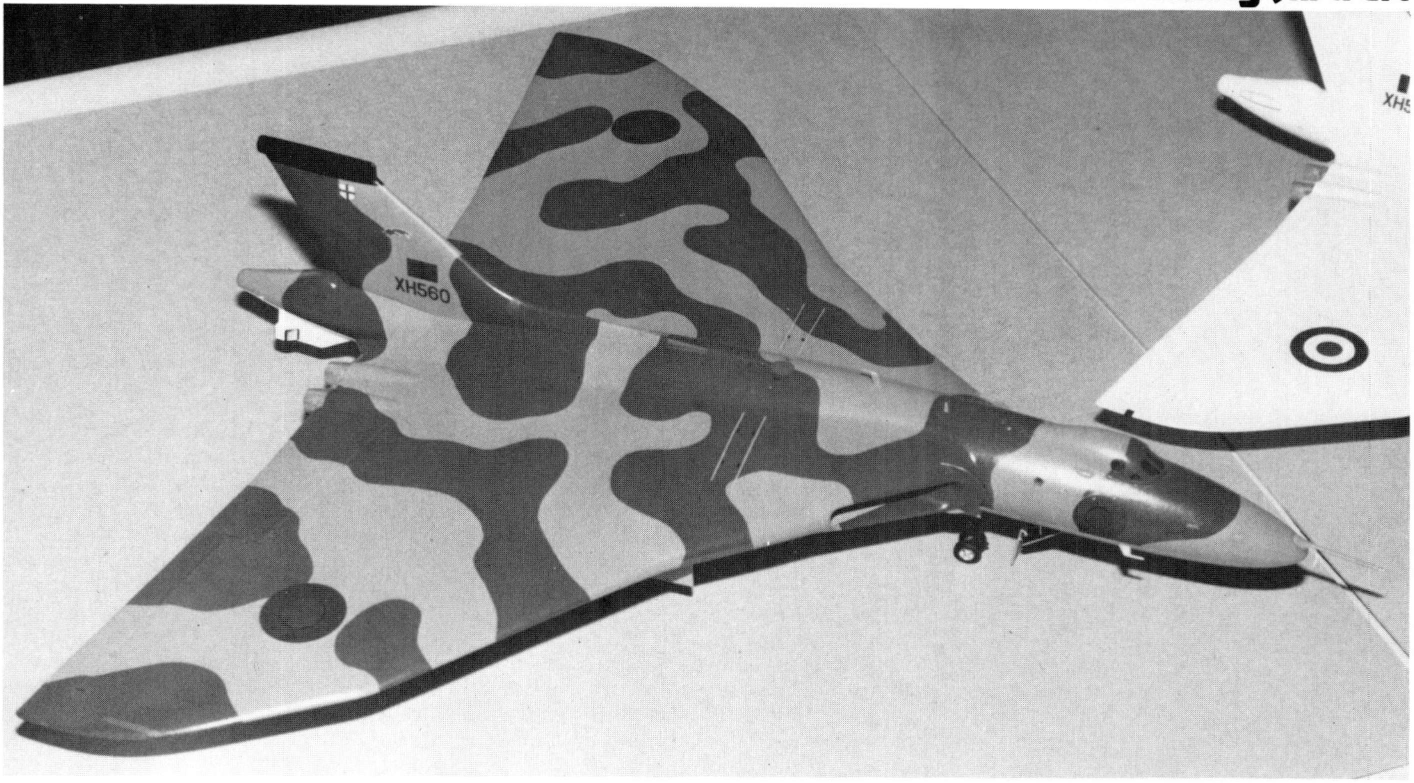

Above:
The Airfix Vulcan converted to a B2K tanker with the aid of a specialist conversion set and Modeldecal markings. Both C Scale and Chota Sahib/Harrier produce white metal parts for the tanker conversion.

Left:
The Aeroclub range of vacformed aircraft kits, mostly to 1/48th scale. Although vacformed kits can be more difficult to build, the arrival of cast metal parts for details such as undercarriage, engines and so on means that there is little more work required to complete even these kits nowadays.

Bottom left:
The Hallam-Vac Westland Welkin, one of the vast range of high-quality vacform kits which are now available. Many (like this one) have cast metal parts for small items such as undercarriage and propellers, which makes construction much easier.
Ron Firth/Pamag Publications

a selection of components that are not needed. Don't throw them away, as sooner or later you will find that they are 'just the job' for some task or other. The advantages of saving spare missiles, bombs and so on is fairly obvious, but wheels, canopies, etc, will also find an eventual use, either within a vacform kit or when pieces are damaged and a substitute part is required quickly. Spares don't suddenly appear overnight; you have to make a conscious effort to keep all your unwanted pieces of plastic, and in time you will be the proud owner of a reserve collection of plastic pieces.

References

Like many other hobbies, with the passage of time you are likely to become either totally bored with the subject or become even more enthusiastic about your hobby and want to pursue the search for 'realism' even further. Whilst many people might be content simply to purchase a kit, assemble the parts and paint it, there is much more to the hobby as you doubtless will have gathered by now. The more interested you become in modelling aircraft, the more important becomes realism and detail. Every modeller's ambition is to create an accurate representation of a real aircraft. Although some might be more concerned with details than others, every modeller wants to make his model as good as he can, and whilst the basic and more advanced modelling skills are the most important abilities needed to achieve this end, there is another factor that can improve the quality of your models considerably, and that is research.

It might be quite possible to look upon model aircraft and real aircraft as two completely different subjects, but the truth is that they are very much connected with each other. There is no point in painting your model and applying decals to represent a particular aircraft if the latter looks nothing like the model in reality. What each modeller must try to achieve is a scaled-down version of the original, which features the same shapes, details and colours. The basic shape and detail is supplied in your kit as are the basic colour scheme and marking details. However, there is absolutely no substitute for first-hand sight of the real aircraft you are portraying. Of course, in almost every instance it would prove impossible to track down any real aircraft you might decide to model. There is one obvious solution to this fact, and that is photography. You must find photographs, and you must collect photographs. Of course, you do not need a library of archive quality colour prints; you can manage perfectly well with magazine illustrations which will show you exactly what an aircraft looks like, how it sits on the runway, how the control surfaces move, what doors and access panels are opened and where, and also just what the precise colours of an aircraft are. You can also determine how the paint surface might have faded in parts, where it might carry repainted patches or where paint has flaked away. You can also see just where any dirt stains might appear, and how noticeable they are. You will also be able to find the odd detail that might have been missed by the kit manufacturer altogether. In fact a good selection of photographs will show any aspect of almost any aircraft you might care to think of.

Where do you find these pictures? Well, there are so many sources it would be impossible to name them all. The obvious places are in books about specific aircraft. Many aircraft are featured in specialist modelling books, which contain large numbers of 'close-up' pictures of the undercarriage, cockpit interior, access panels and doors, instrument bay interiors and so on. These publications are aimed specifically at the modeller who needs to know exactly what an aircraft looks like. Modelling magazines regularly feature close-up photographs of many aircraft, together with drawings of internal structures, cockpit layouts, etc. Model magazines will also provide you with a regular supply of colour scheme information on many subjects, give you modelling advice, demonstrate how to build specific models,and keep you up to date with the latest kits and accessories that are available. There is no substitute for a regular supply of modelling publications and a subscription to at least one is a wise step. If you can afford to spend a little more on magazines you should also consider buying aviation titles, as these will often include plenty of good photographic references that are bound to be useful at some time.

An even more useful step would be to join a modelling club where you could meet fellow modellers and learn more about your hobby from others who will have shared your experiences. There are many local clubs around the country, and there is also the International Plastic Modellers' Society which has branches all around the

Above:
The Revell P-38M Lightning has been carefully detailed by cutting open some access panels and detailing their interiors. Good reference photographs are essential for finding details of such places.

Left:
A good close-up photograph can reveal important details that are useful when building a scale replica. In this view the underside of a Jaguar GR1's wing can be seen in detail and the intricate trailing edge flap arrangement is clearly visible. Without a photograph it would be very difficult to try and incorporate these details on a model.

Below:
With even a small pocket camera, useful close-up photographs can be obtained at any air show. In this picture the intricate flap detail of a Tornado can be seen. A good selection of such illustrations are regularly included in most modelling magazines.

Above:
A close look at the upper surface of a Jaguar wing shows the complex nature of the trailing edge flaps.

world. The UK branch has a large range of clubs scattered around the country, and by joining the IPMS you can soon find out where your local club meets. IPMS produces a bi-monthly magazine which is free to every member, and contains a large variety of modelling information. IPMS also holds many exhibitions around the country, including the biggest plastic modelling exhibition held in the UK each year, where the country's top modellers annually show their latest creations to their many admirers. You can find details

Above right:
A good collection of aviation books and magazines will reveal many useful details on all types of aircraft. There are so many titles to choose from that any particular aircraft is likely to be covered in great detail in one publication or another.

Right:
Modelling magazines are published regularly in both the UK and elsewhere, the range of topics covered being almost limitless. The more magazines you can collect, the better your handy references will be.

Below:
There is an ever-expanding range of small-run enthusiast publications that cover endless ranges of aviation and modelling subjects. Seen here are some World War 1 magazines and books that are available.

Below right:
The International Plastic Modellers' Society is a world-wide group of modellers who regularly produce national journals filled with modelling information. The UK branch produces a bi-monthly magazine — as do many other countries — copies of which are available to any IPMS member.

about joining IPMS in any modelling magazine.

A further source of reference material is to take your own photographs, by visiting airports and air shows. If you are interested in airliners you can easily obtain shots of aircraft at your nearest airport as they come and go. If you can manage to reach Heathrow you will find possibly the greatest variety of airliners to be found anywhere in the world, so there is a whole collection of aircraft just waiting to be examined there each day. Of course you cannot really get too close to any airliner, so you would probably need a telephoto lens to obtain close-up photographs. However, a pair of binoculars and a sketch pad will give a similar result.

If your interest is in military aircraft it is possible to take detail photographs with a telephoto lens from the perimeter of any military airfield. It must be said, however, that considerable care must be taken and common sense used because the military authorities are not too keen on any people lurking close to the edge of their airfields, and will often ask photographers to leave. They have even been known to confiscate films (and cameras!). More importantly, should you venture abroad, many countries will arrest anyone attempting to photograph military aircraft, so be warned! There is a much safer and more effective way of taking your own photographs of military aircraft, and that is by going to air shows. Here you will be free to photograph any aircraft you can see, many of which will be just inches away and thus allow even the owners of pocket cameras to obtain some really useful reference shots of aircraft details. There are also many aviation museums to be found, all of which contain a whole range of aircraft available for examination throughout the year (check the opening times

Above:
A Spitfire with a difference. There are so many colour scheme and markings possibilities for this famous aircraft that one is only limited by one's memory or imagination! Here is a little-publicised American scheme. Note the weathering effect on the wing inboard section and fuselage, which suggest chipped or scuffed paintwork.

Above right:
If the colour scheme possibilities are not enough, you can physically alter a basic Spitfire into a variety of versions, in this case a high-altitude mark with extended wing tips. Plastic card and filler are the main requirements.

Below:
An airliner, but in the 'military' $^1/_{72}$nd scale. The kits of the C-47/DC3 Dakota (produced by Esci, Italeri and Revell) can easily be changed into civil versions. In this case the markings have been hand-painted.

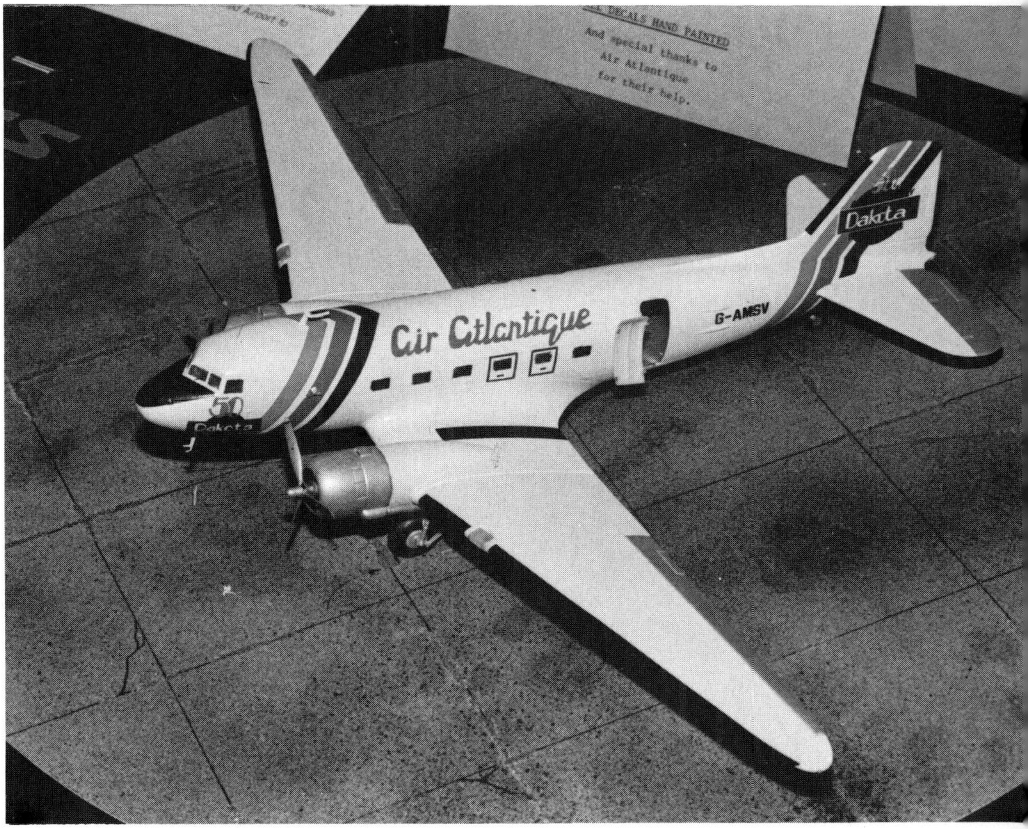

before you go, though!). Researching references will enhance your hobby and provide you with plenty of information which in turn will make a better model: many modellers find that the search for information can be as rewarding as building the model itself. The basic rule is to 'know your subject'. Before you build any kit, try and become as familiar with it as possible. Find references to the subject, and if you cannot afford to take photographs or even buy magazines, go to your local library where a selection of books will always be available. Do not forget jumble sales, too, where magazines can often be picked up cheaply. Also keep an eye open for model exhibitions. There is likely to be at least one near you at some time during the year, and they are always worth visiting, not only for picking up bargains but also for meeting other modellers who can pass on many useful tips.

Right:
Swedish selection: a small collection of Swedish aircraft, which could be expanded to limitless proportions. There are many other themes to which a collection could be built.

Below:
Two de Havilland Mosquitos, both to 1/72nd scale, with a later aircraft used for similar purposes — the Canberra. The basic Airfix Canberra has been modified, by the addition of a solid (as opposed to a clear) nose section, and a new colour scheme applied.

Below right:
Two Lincolns made from the Airfix Lancaster kit.

Bottom:
An example of the 1/72nd scale kit of the Super Etendard produced by Heller. On the port wing is a long range fuel tank; the starboard wing carries an Exocet missile (provided in the kit).